thin 🌀 _threads_

LIFE CHANGING MOMENTS

Real Stories
of Life Changing Moments

COMPILED BY

STACEY K. BATTAT

kiwi·technologies
Woodbridge, Connecticut

Thin Threads: Real Stories of Life Changing Moments

The classic edition

Copyright 2010 Kiwi Publishing, Inc.
Published by: Kiwi Publishing, Inc., a subsidiary of Kiwi Technologies
Post Office Box 3852
Woodbridge CT 06525
info@kiwipublishing.com
www.kiwipublishing.com
866-836-7913

ISBN 978-0-9800564-5-7

First Edition: January, 2010
Printed in the United States

Dedication

I DEDICATE THIS BOOK to countless people: The authors and future authors of Thin Threads® stories, for sharing life experiences that will touch other people's lives and reach far and wide. I dedicate it to my children, Yoni, Sivan, and Nadav who are truly my pride, joy, and inspiration.

Special thanks to my sister, Stephanie, for her guidance, wisdom and insights which have always surpassed her years, and for her invaluable editorial mind. A huge thank you to my friend and mentor Joyce, who continues to be integral in helping me focus my thoughts through the words that will help convey the message of *Thin Threads* in the venues and to the people to whom I speak. I also thank our many friends and colleagues who served as the first unofficial reading "advisory board."

The ultimate dedication of this book, however, is to my partner in business, love and life. We share so many passions and were blessed to take our bright lights and create an even stronger force together. If I am the eyes, ears, heart and face of the *Thin Threads* message, it is truly Eitan who is the creative mind behind it. He ties all the threads together.

Contents

Preface

YOGI BERRA ONCE said, "When you come to a fork in the road, take it."

Have you ever encountered a fork in the road? Perhaps a door was opened and it led you down an unexpected pathway to a new beginning. Perhaps it was when you found yourself in a strange place or had a fateful interaction with a total stranger. You get the idea.

Each of us has these *thin thread* moments—moments when a decision we made, or even a small detour in our lives, laid before us a brand-new path. Sometimes we recognize them instantly. Sometimes it takes weeks, years, even decades to identify those defining moments. By unraveling thin threads and sharing them in the form of short stories, the Thin Thread® book series offers you, our readers, the chance to become more present to the openings in your *own* lives.

My own life story is composed of such *thin threads*. One of my first jobs was as a field producer for a cable TV show, where I was honored to interview people and uncover the stories behind their passions. Many times the story took me off track, and when it did, I followed it. My life has always been a lot like that; if there was a sign that was truly calling my name, I listened. My ultimate career and my beloved husband and partner, and my best friend, were uncovered

VII

by surprise. In fact, the banner of my life could read "not all who wander are lost."

Other people approach diversions differently. Among the thousands of people who've submitted stories, I have encountered numerous approaches to dealing with the detours and setbacks that we all experience. Yet what they all share is the realization that it is in these moments that we may find magic, signs of where the road should take us.

Nowadays, after hearing from the many who have submitted their stories and experiences of life-changing moments, I am even more open to what is calling me. You can be too!

I hope that the stories you are about to read take you on a journey of self-reflection, inspiration and motivation. By reading them you may recognize the strands that weave magic in your own life, and be more open to what is calling you. A very wise person once said "sometimes in the wind of change we find our true direction." Are you ready to expect the unexpected? Let the journey begin!

Stacey K. Battat

Introduction

WHEN I READ one of the stories where people recon-
nect, "Reach Out Before It's Too Late," about a
middle-aged woman named Maureen racing to the bedside
of her childhood friend, I didn't know it would change my
life. But after reading it, I decided to look up a few of my very
close high school and college buddies, whom I had lost contact
with. I had not spoken with Sam in more than a decade, and
discovered he had lost his mom, and had been divorced and
then remarried during that time. When we finally recon-
nected in person, we both found our reunion to be invigorat-
ing. We inspired each other with the idea of connecting our
spouses and families, opening new ways to share dreams we
found exciting, and we reunited with a stronger bond than
we had back in high school.

My daughter and I met a Darfurian refugee named Alfidel
on a train ride. His stories changed our lives forever, and my
daughter kept in touch with him and invited him to share
his story with 1,800 students at her high school. Through
our connections, he is now speaking at schools all over the
Northeast. You never know where or when you'll meet the
people who will have the biggest impact on your lives, or the
lives of your community and beyond.

You might find these stories so inspiring that you will read this book all in one sitting. But even if you just flip open to a random story, you will be amazed at how it seems to apply to your life, right here, right now. Each story has elements that will enlighten you and motivate you. There is always a reason you open a page to a certain place, even if it's not what you expected.

These stories all show how connected we are with one another in the fabric of life ... how we are one another's lifelines. The threads alone are fragile, but they become stronger as we support one another in the universe.

In the story "Lose Your Mind," Maurice was never happy as a Wall Street trader; now he runs a children's charity. His salary is a small fraction of what it once was, but he is a lot happier and feels far more fulfilled. His thin thread took the form of a sick boy in a hospital, someone he'd never met before.

"Getting fired from Apple was the best thing that could have ever happened to me," said Steve Jobs, years ago. "The heaviness of being successful was replaced by the lightness of being a beginner again, less sure about everything. It freed me to enter one of the most creative periods of my life." (He started Pixar Pictures soon after.)

My friend Rita read "Unforeseen Turn" and realized that her own recovery time after a terrible car accident offered her the chance to renew her original love of writing, and she is now publishing her songs and poetry in a multitude of forums. Having come through a year of challenges, she had made her writing essential to her well-being and self-expression.

In times long gone, when we confronted challenging times, our family and friends were always by our side telling us stories to help guide us on our way. That's how you can think of this book: stories from people who have lessons to share. These are the lessons you didn't know you needed. They appeal to us because they have a hidden meaning in our own lives that becomes more evident as we read.

We are all affected by the events of others. Here are the answers, if you're wondering "What's next in my life?" or "How can I make the right decision?" It may not seem obvious at first. But if life's answers were obvious, we wouldn't need inspiration from other people. Read just one story, and you'll see what I mean. I hope you will share them with the people who mean the most to you.

Stacey K. Battat

Thin Threads

A Funny Thing Happened
on the Way to the Library

Finding a mission in life through laughter

Joyce M. Saltman

WITH THE POSSIBLE exception of my earlobes, there is nothing about me that is thin. *Thin* is not even a word that I can relate to, yet when I heard about the concept of *thin threads*, I was enthralled. This was not to be a collection of worn-out jeans, or sewing notions, or any of the other commonly understood meanings of "threads," thin or otherwise. This was to be a celebration of life-changing events of "real" people; the exploration of those magic moments that are usually unplanned and unexpected and have the power to change lives. Though unexceptional in appearance, these *thin threads* can tie together an everyday situation or simple coincidence and turn the episode into a profound and life-altering event. I never imagined that anything "thin" could have such significance!

If each of us were to closely examine our lives, we would probably see the seeds, if not the fruition, of many such threads. My own life-changing incident occurred shortly after my marriage to a wonderful man, who had no idea how crazy (or at least, gutsy!) I really was.

When Kopi first met me, I was a professor of Special Education at Southern Connecticut State University and a psychotherapist with a private practice in Cheshire. Having recently divorced my husband of 15 years, I was doing stand-up comedy with three male acquaintances on Monday nights at a local restaurant as a "between husbands" activity. I had no difficulty getting material because my life provided more than the requisite number of funny stories. I focused on my mom, my students, and my dates, creating stories from my experiences, for example, about the one who was so young that instead of sleeping together, we were taking naps together, and so on. It seemed as though my life was designed perfectly to offer amusement to others!

Fortunately for me, at that same time the Cheshire library was planning a series on healing, and they had already obtained speakers to lecture about massage, tai chi, and other similar topics. When Maria Poirier, the series coordinator, called me, she said, "We know you are a lecturer, a therapist, and a comedienne. Would you be willing to give a talk on the therapeutic benefits of laughter?" Needless to say, I agreed to do so.

That evening, Kopi returned from playing principal at a private, very conservative K-8 school, and I greeted him with, "Honey, I got a call from the Cheshire library, and I'm going to give a lecture there in September!" My excitement was contagious, and Kopi eagerly asked what I was going to be lecturing about. I responded, "I will be speaking about the therapeutic benefits of laughter," to which he said, "Honey, that's wonderful. What do you know about that?" In my offhanded way, I said, "Nothing. But I know it's true, and I know how to read!!!"

As luck would have it, the Cheshire Library sent its calendar of upcoming events to all the local papers. My first lecture, on what has now become my favorite topic, was covered by the *Waterbury Republican*, the *Hartford Courant* (which sent a photographer and reporter to the actual lecture!), and the *New Haven Register*. By the next morning, my life was changed forever. I began getting phone calls from insurance companies, state agencies, schools, and corporations. Overnight, as if by magic, I had become what my friend Peter always called me: world famous in Connecticut!

I guess one could say that the rest is history. It has been 25 years since that first talk, and I have given the lecture several thousand times in the United States, Canada, Australia, England, Norway, Italy, Luxembourg, and Japan. I have been able to give nearly one million dollars to my favorite charities and have met celebrities I never would have encountered if not for the opportunities that being a public speaker has provided. As a great believer in the premise that we all are here on earth to help repair the world, I am convinced that being able to help people "lighten up" is a major part of the gift I have been given. My mission in life has largely been realized as a result of this one *thin thread*.

Wishes Do Come True

When a penny for your thought brings abundance

Elizabeth Anne Hill

As told by Cindy Marten

I WAS BORN IN Chicago, Illinois, on October 3, 1966, and was a healthy baby girl in all respects. My parents, Marian and Roger, were very young at the time and did not feel that they could provide the kind of home that a newborn required. They consequently made the gut-wrenching decision to give me up for adoption only five days after my birth. Fortunately for me, they found a loving family that could raise me the way my parents would have wanted.

Ever since I can remember, I knew that I was adopted. I had a wonderful family and was a happy, secure kid, but I frequently thought about my birth mother. I knew that my biological father had been killed in a motorcycle accident a few years after my birth, so as a young child, I made a wish that someday my birth mother would come find me.

My brother Charlie was diagnosed with intellectual challenges, and my adoptive parents discovered that California offered better social services and education for someone with his needs. So we moved to San Diego when I was ten years old. Being a few years older than Charlie, I became his guide and mentor, and from my experiences helping him, I knew I was going to become a teacher one day.

As I grew older, I would think of my birth mother more and more. By the spring of 2002, my wish to connect with her became stronger than ever. By this time I was blessed with a wonderful husband and son and my dream job as a vice-principal at Central Elementary School in San Diego. But I knew that out there somewhere lived a woman who had given me up because she wanted more for me. I felt that she should have the honor of knowing how well I was doing, how happy my life was, and how many young lives I was touching in my work.

I picked up a book called *And Then She Found Me*, by Eleanor Lipman. It was a novel about an adoptee eventually found by her birth mother. I was stunned by the similarities between the fictitious story and my own life. The main character was born in Chicago, Illinois, was given up for adoption to a Jewish family, and had later become a teacher.

The novel prompted me to research an adoption website, where I discovered no listings that matched my date of birth. I entered my birth information on the site and in time forgot all about it.

Four years later, just a few months before my fortieth birthday, I received an unexpected email from the adoption website. At first I thought it was just junk mail, but when I opened the email, I read, "Dear Cindy, I registered on your site this morning, and based on the information you provided we seem to be a match."

I sat in stunned silence, barely breathing. I read on. "I am jumping out of my skin with anticipation, so I decided to email you right away. My name is Marian and I hope and pray that I am your birth mother."

After exchanging numerous emails and phone calls, we determined that she was indeed my birth mother, so I decided to fly to Chicago to meet her. As I was leaving school for the airport, I saw a penny lying on the ground. I picked it up and put it in my pocket.

I arrived in Chicago and drove to the hotel where we planned to meet. The moment finally arrived. When I saw her walking toward me, I realized that my lifelong dream was finally becoming a reality. We were both choked with emotion as we embraced, and we had so many things to say to each other. We found a coffee shop where we could talk, and as I looked down on the ground near our table, I saw three pennies. "Oh, more lucky pennies," I thought and put them in my pocket. I had always believed in making wishes, but at that moment I *knew* that wishes really do come true.

When I returned to work after my life-changing trip, I found pennies and other coins everywhere. With such good fortune, I began a campaign to teach our students how to believe in their own wishes. I added the phrase "Dream Big" to our school motto. The kids loved the addition and chanted, "Work Hard, Be Kind, Dream Big!" I knew that I had established all the components for a successful school, but the one thing that had been missing was a sense of belief. The kids needed to believe in something in order to see it come true.

The children and teachers were very excited about all the pennies I was collecting, and they began finding them everywhere as well—all over the school, in parks, alleys, and grocery stores. We were all mesmerized by this occurrence, because it was uncommon to find money lying around in such a poor neighborhood.

The kids made "dream jars," and we put one in each classroom. Every day, several children came running excitedly toward me, shouting, "Mrs. Martin! Mrs. Martin! I found a penny!" Together we would go into the nearest classroom, and I would encourage each child to make a wish and drop the penny in the jar.

Central Elementary is classified as a 100 percent *Title One* school, which means that virtually all of the children are considered socially and economically disadvantaged and at risk for poor school performance. Eighty-five percent of them speak English as a second language, and many have great difficulty on standardized state tests.

I insisted that the students understood that it didn't matter where they came from or what their family life was like. They could do well in school and could be anything they wanted to be. After we added "Dream Big" to our school motto and included dream jars in the classrooms, we received an unexpected gift.

Our school-wide proficiency score rose from 18 percent to 29 percent, and our English learners showed an enormous jump in test scores from a proficiency rate of just 10 percent to 26 percent.

Ever since I have been at Central Elementary we have experienced steady growth, but a jump in scores that large could be attributed to only one fact: the children believed, as I still believe, that wishes really do come true.

Eulogy Party

A final gift for friends

Joseph Civitella

W ALLY RECEIVED THE message from his secretary, who had been given the message by the doctor's assistant. The biopsy results were back. The next morning, he presented himself at the medical office, where he was promptly led to a private examining room.

"Wally," began the doctor, "I'm afraid the news is not good." No amount of bravura could prevent the sinking feeling Wally felt.

"Tell it to me like it is, doc. No use sugarcoating it."

The doctor nodded. "You have cancer of the liver . . . and it's already at an advanced stage." Wally gazed at the doctor and braced himself for what was to come next.

"And that means?"

"Unfortunately, it means that we can't do anything to help you at this point."

His heart and mind raced in a mad rush to find something other than the obvious conclusion to the diagnosis. There was nothing else. "How long do I have?"

"Best-case scenario . . . six months."

"And worst-case scenario?"

11

"Maybe three months."

Wally closed his eyes and heard only silence. In his mind's eye he saw an image of his wife and two children. How was he going to tell them? What would become of them? When would be the last time he could hug them?

He returned home and found his wife in their bedroom, sorting through clothes in the walk-in closet. She knew that something was wrong with him, but he had not told her about the biopsy. He asked her to sit on the edge of the bed with him. "Honey, we need to talk." His wife looked at him with a perplexed expression.

"The last time I heard a man start a conversation like that, he broke up with me."

He had always loved her sense of humor, and despite his despair, he smiled at her and took her hand.

"What is it, sweetie?" she asked. "Your hand is trembling."

He couldn't answer and began crying. They had a very open relationship and could say anything to each other when the need arose as long as it was the truth, the whole truth, and nothing but the truth.

"I don't know how to say this in a way that will make it easier for you to hear, so I'll say it whatever way it comes out, okay?"

"Sweetie, you're scaring me." Wally cleared his throat and held her hand tighter.

"Remember when I went to the doctor for my checkup?"

"Yeah."

He hesitated. "What I didn't tell you is that he ran some tests."

She stared blankly at him. "What kind of tests?"

"A biopsy," he said softly as tears inundated his eyes.

"What?" she whispered.

His voice broke. "I have liver cancer, honey."

"No!"

He held her gaze. "And it's inoperable."

"No!" She started crying as well.

There was nothing else that needed to be said. They simply held each other for the longest time and slept in each other's arms that night as they had often done when they first were married 22 years earlier. Their tears blended into a river of sadness over their pillows. He whispered in her ear, "I want to enjoy every day with you as if it's my first and my last."

She replied softly, "I love you so much."

Over the ensuing weeks, Wally put all his affairs in order and made the necessary financial arrangements for his family. Among all the loose ends that he tied up, one thread kept dangling in his consciousness. Because of his faith in love that is deep and true, he wanted the people around him to celebrate his life instead of mourning his premature death.

He had always been the imaginative type, but he had never thought about how he would die or how he would like to be remembered. He took hold of that last dangling thread and wove it into a new rite of passage in the form of a pre-death wake. But instead of calling it a wake, he called it a Eulogy Party.

Wally booked a good friend's restaurant for a Thursday evening and invited all the significant people in his life. While he sat in a comfortable chair among all the guests, he encouraged each of them to stand at the podium and deliver a eulogy as though Wally had already passed away.

He heard the many wonderful stories and sentiments that people wanted to share with him. Many guests were unable to contain their emotions and cried while reading a text they had written. Others recalled the practical jokes that Wally had played on them or that they had played on Wally. They regretted that they hadn't laughed more. And one dear friend simply stood at the podium and remained silent while gazing at Wally. Finally, all he said was, "I never noticed before how beautiful you are."

Wally responded in kind to each one of his guests, telling them what he appreciated about them. And at the end of the event, he stood at the podium and read a poem.

My Echo

When I die and my body is in its final resting place,
Please bring children to my wake to look upon my face,
Tell them that I am sleeping on this bed in the house of God.
When they ask if I am happy, smile and answer with a nod,
You see my body and think that it is dead, but I am not gone,
I am living with the angels of childhood spirits in eternal dawn,
Where a smile is sincere, a kiss is genuine,
And love is pure, and the bond between us can never break; it's
  divinely secure.

I can also live in your heart if you choose to have me there,
I can live in your memory if you choose to keep me there,
I can live with your soul if you choose to share it with me,
I can live with your spirit if you will be truthful with me,
I am dead only to the extent that you allow me to die,
You look at my body, it is still, but don't say goodbye,
Look, listen and touch with all the senses of your soul,
You will see, hear and touch what you know to be whole,
I can never die or be gone from you if you allow me to live,
Not with you, but within you, and freely receive what I give,
Like the first cry of a newborn child to announce its birth,
My echo, it lives in the soft breeze, from the ocean to earth.

Wally passed away only weeks later with no regrets about having left something unsaid or unheard. Many tears of sadness were shed at his funeral, but many tears of joy were shed as well. Wally had the foresight and wisdom to help everyone create one last, enduring memory. He chose to die with grace and dignity, a Eulogy Party as his parting legacy.

Touchdown

First and ten from the lifeline

Claudia D'Souza

YOUR LIFE CAN change in a split second—irrevocably and resolutely. It's not a thought that we dwell on as we race through endless busy days. It was not a thought Canadian Football League (CFL) hero Terry Evanshen entertained in his first life.

When Evanshen's body was catapulted backward through his jeep window one shining July evening in 1988, he no longer knew what "time" was. He no longer knew who he was. Before the accident in 1988, Evanshen, a CFL Hall of Famer, had come a long way from the slum near Montreal where he was raised with twelve siblings. Evanshen's brilliant fourteen-year career as a wide receiver was behind him, but he had a Grey Cup ring, a successful career as a salesman, his loving wife, Lorraine, three beautiful daughters, and an 1867 home and horse farm in Brooklin, northeast of Toronto.

Driving home to fire up the barbecue that July night, Evanshen was looking forward to telling his family about his successful business trip in Europe. But a van racing through a red light broke his reverie with the force of a small bomb. T-boned at an intersection, Evanshen's jeep flew up in the air, landed, and then rolled. The impact ripped his seatbelt from its hoist and propelled him backward through the rear window. His shattered body lay face down and motionless on the roadside.

Two weeks and numerous operations later, Evanshen emerged from a deep and puzzling coma with absolutely no memory of his first forty-four years. Three severe complications were to blame. The velocity of the crash had battered his brain against his skull (called diffuse axonal injury, or DAI), killing millions of brain cells. Oxygen deprivation due to broken ribs and a collapsed lung destroyed millions of message-sending neurons, and he suffered frontal lobe damage. Left with retrograde amnesia (permanent loss of long-term memory) and impaired short-term memory, Evanshen's life became a virtual clean slate. "I didn't know my wife and children. I didn't know what marriage was or a kiss or a hug. I just existed," he said. "I was like a two-year-old. I had to relearn toilet training, how to walk, talk, and tie my shoes. I was back at the starting point."

Reprogramming himself to learn basic life tasks was a major struggle. But the frontal lobe is the control center of concentration, memory, and behavior. For years, Lorraine and the children learned a great deal about tolerance, patience, and persistence while coping with a man who no longer recognized them. Being irritable, rude, impatient, and indifferent, he was prone to fits of rage and depression. He no longer had a sense of humor, and his caring, affectionate, sensitive nature seemed gone forever.

"I was in a fog. I didn't care about anything," he said. "I would yell 'Don't tell me what to do!' I didn't even know I was yelling. If it wasn't for the love of my family, I'd be in a psychiatric ward."

Evanshen largely credits Lorraine with keeping him sane and on a forward path. "She is 100 percent my safety net," he says. As the years went by, he made progress as he began performing basic, daily tasks. But he still can't store the episodic memories of his life for longer than a few days. He uses sticky notes to remind himself of the Ws—*what, where, when, who, and why*—when he's going about his day.

But Evanshen's determination and fearlessness were inborn from his scrappy childhood in a tough neighborhood and largely contributed to his success on the football field. That part of him somehow survived, and he refused to give up trying to regain as much of his former self as he could. He began giving motivational talks in the late 1990s entitled "Seize the Day." He still delivers these talks to this day. A charismatic speaker, he touches his audience with his honesty and tremendous will to survive.

Acclaimed Canadian author the late June Callwood's twenty-ninth book, *The Man Who Lost Himself,* chronicles Evanshen's heroic and fascinating triumph over brain damage and total memory loss. It was made into a TV movie of the same name starring David James Elliott of *JAG* fame and later sold to the Lifetime Network, which distributed it to more than 20 countries. Every time it airs, Evanshen receives emails from admiring fans around the world. "What still defined him was his courage and determination to succeed—his unwillingness to concede failure," Callwood noted during her book tour with Evanshen in 2000. "He's impatient and very tough on himself, but he's more and more in control." Callwood admitted she almost turned down the challenge of writing about Evanshen's journey. "I declined the offer at first," she said. "I didn't know whether I could write a book about a man with no memory. But I realized that I had to try to understand. It was my challenge as a journalist." These days there are few outward clues of his bitter, desperate struggle to find himself. He looks perhaps fifty, but he's sixty-four and works out regularly at the gym to maintain his physique.

He enjoys doting on his five grandchildren, who call him "papa." But he finds it difficult to talk about the loss of his youngest daughter, Jennifer. She died in 2001 from a brain tumor that rendered her blind in her last days. However, he has come to accept it.

Reflecting on his life, Evanshen acknowledges that, given his injuries, he should have died in the accident—his *thin thread*. But he believes that he's still here to help others through their own struggles and to inspire them to always reach higher. "I was meant to live," he says simply. "I have no regrets about living on. I entertain possibilities in each person. I ask them whether they are really the best person they can be for themselves and for those around them. I live each day like it's my last and remind others how little we appreciate our time. The good Lord has given us today; forget about tomorrow. Enjoy each and every moment."

The Tip

A gift's true value
may take years to be realized

Maris L. Franco

YEARS AGO, I waited tables at a breakfast diner. It was one of those old-fashioned eateries that were home to countless early birds, who were there at 6:00 A.M. for their daily eggs, grits, and toast. The other waitresses and I did everything by hand, and by the end of my ten-hour shift, I was exhausted.

One Saturday afternoon, I was getting ready to head home after refilling all of my salt and pepper shakers and making sure that the ketchup bottles were wiped clean. I had one final table to close out before collecting my tips. The table was a "two-top" as we called it—a small booth presently inhabited by two elderly gentlemen. The men had not been particularly nice while I served their lunches, but I kept a smile on my face and tried to be as obliging as I could. After I had taken their dishes away, I asked whether they were ready for their check. "Not yet," they replied.

Half an hour went by, so I returned to their table and politely asked, "Sir, may I bring you your check?"

The man to my left answered, "When we're ready to leave, we'll let you know."

Finally, after an hour and a half, the two men signaled me over and asked for their check. This was certainly not the first time that a patron had tested my patience, but by this point, any shred of hospitality that I had left was lost in my exhaustion. I placed the tab on the table and walked away, feeling sure that they would understand my subtle hint. After an agonizing ten minutes, one of the men called for me once more.

"Oh great," I said to myself. "Now there's a problem with the bill." I shuffled back to their table and asked,

"Is there something wrong with your check?"

"No, no," he replied. "Everything's fine. Just wanted to let you know that we left you the best tip you'll ever get."

"Well thank you for your generosity," I replied, ashamed at my own impatience. After all, these two old friends had obviously been enjoying themselves.

After the men left, I went over to clear off their table and collect my tip. To my amazement, a folded two-dollar bill lay underneath a half-empty water glass. I was furious! After making me wait all that time and then assuring me that my tip would be great, these guys had the nerve to leave me a two-dollar tip? But then again, two-dollar bills were rare, and some people might have been thrilled with this new find; however, I was not one of those people. I finished clearing off the table, grabbed my coat, and stormed out, berating myself for holding onto the table for a measly two dollars instead of handing it over to a co-worker.

As time went by, I found the humor in the situation. Although not a collector of money, I could never bring myself to spend that two-dollar bill. Instead, I viewed it as a relic of my "rite of passage" into the harshness of reality, and I kept it in the clear plastic pocket in my wallet. In fact, any time I purchased a new wallet, I made sure that it had a similar clear pocket just big enough to hold the "best tip that I had ever gotten."

While out watching baseball with friends one night at a local bar, I met a handsome young man. He and I hit it off right away and wound up chatting all night. Throughout the evening, he had asked whether he could see me again. I replied, "I'm not sure, yet." I just was not the type to make plans with a complete stranger, either. As the night came to a close, we asked for our bills from our waitress. As she presented my new friend with his tab, he opened his wallet, revealing a neatly folded two-dollar bill in a small, clear pocket. Stunned, I opened my wallet and showed him the inside. There we sat, staring at each other and laughing in disbelief.

Needless to say, I finally accepted the man's request for a date. Three years later, I am still thrilled that I did. Yet every now and then, I can't help but feel grateful when I think about those two old men who kept me at work all those years ago. They surely did leave me with the greatest tip that I ever got—to be thankful for even the smallest and seemingly insignificant gifts I receive because their true value may reveal themselves to be much more than meets the eye.

The Tella-Jerusalem Project

When climbing for a cause is not the only cause

Bethany Garfield

As told by Eitan Battat

A T AN EARLY hour of the night, I lay still on the cold ground with my heart racing. "This is it," I thought. "I'm going to die here."

I was petrified that my worst fear had come true. After the first day of climbing Mount Kilimanjaro in Tanzania my heart might be giving out. At the age of fifty and with little climbing experience, this was not an unrealistic thought. As I contemplated whether to wake up my tent mate and alert him to a situation he could do little about, or simply have the Connecticut attorney find "my dead body" in the morning, I heard a woman's scream from the neighboring tent. Ignoring my own state of terror, I ran to her aid. As I comforted the shaken woman, it was apparent that she was experiencing the same anxiety and fear I was. "I realized that she was having a panic attack,and that I was about to have one too. She was sent to tell me, 'Hey, be cool.'"

During this moment as I consoled my fellow climber, I overcame my fears. I had documented thirty-eight worries in a written list prior to the climb, and this event led me to realize once and for all that all fears were just illusions.

23

I continued the climb, confident that I would make it to the top, and I did—first to Stella Point and then to the highest summit, Uhuru Peak, at an elevation of 19,566 feet. Twenty other climbers from around the world and I made the six-day journey up Kilimanjaro as a fundraising effort for the Make-a-Wish International Foundation.

I admit that I wanted nothing to do with the climb at first. It was "peer pressure" from my friend Avi, co-founder of Make-a-Wish-Israel, that forced me up the Tanzanian mountain. Despite my initial reluctance, however, the climb was well worth it. But while the climb itself was an incredible experience filled with beautiful scenery and lessons learned, it was where I went afterward that brought me true fulfillment.

After returning to the Keys Hotel in Moshi, Tanzania, two climbers and I wanted to continue our journey further to meet the people of Tanzania. We didn't want to just walk around and go shopping; we wanted to experience life in an actual Tanzanian village.

We began the search for a willing escort at 8 A.M. on the last morning of our stay in Tanzania, knowing full well that our plane was departing at midnight that evening. Our itinerary gave us a short window of time to find what we were looking for. We tried with all our resources to locate a cab or tour guide to take us to a non-tourist destination. Hours passed, and we were unable to find anyone who could escort us to a Tanzanian village:

We were disappointed and disheartened. As we discussed whether to give up our search, I felt a tap on my shoulder. "I hear that you're looking for somebody to drive you around," the man said. "I am a doctor around here. I would love to show you around, and you don't have to pay me. I want to show you a few things."

The man who became our tour guide was Dr. Fidelis. His wife was the sales director for the hotel. Thrilled by this unexpected offer, we crawled into Dr. Fidelis's small Toyota and set off for the village of Tella. "I'm going to take you to the village where I was born," the doctor told us.

But before taking us to Tella, Dr. Fidelis drove to a market outside the small town. He told us that this market was a major lifeline for the village of Tella. When it rained, the road to the market was washed out, leaving many women—who regularly made the four-mile walk to exchange baskets of fruit at the market—without food for their families until the rain stopped and the road reopened. Seeing the sights of the market and hearing the stories, the three of us felt we had achieved our goal—we were entering a new world in Tanzania. After snapping some pictures of townspeople at the market, we jumped back in the car and continued our journey.

As Dr. Fidelis drove us toward the center of Tella, children from the village started running after our car. I don't think that the kids had ever seen a white man before, because they were running behind the car screaming, "Wazungu! Wazungu!" or Swahili for "white man."

The roads were hardly roads at all, and the children dodged several potholes as they ran after the car. They followed the car until it reached The Tella Primary School, where Dr. Fidelis had been a student as a child. We were given a tour of the facility and learned that the school was experiencing a shortage of sugar. The head priest told them that an increase in sugar could help feed the students and possibly allow more children to attend. We immediately donated thirty dollars, which would purchase fifty kilos of sugar.

While the money was nothing to us, the people at the school were very grateful. The donation was received as a large gesture by the children and faculty of the school. Shortly after the priest was informed of the gift, the school's three hundred students lined up in rows outside. Then with smiling faces, they began to sing the Tanzanian National Anthem.

It was a very emotional moment for me to see those kids singing because I thought about my own children, and I missed them very much. The students sang while the three of us (all dads) stood there crying. As I watched the young Tanzanian students sing in appreciation, I decided at that moment that I was going to help the people at this school as much as I could.

The living conditions for the students were very different from those of many American children. Most homes were single-parent families because AIDS or other diseases had claimed the life of a child's mother or father. There was no electricity, and whole families were sleeping on the floors in their homes. I became fascinated with how little the children of Tella had but how happy they were despite their lack of luxuries.

I realized that this part of the world was full of people trying to make a good life for themselves. And I also realized that many of us in the United States did not appreciate the luxuries we enjoyed, such as running water, electricity, computers, and so on. Surely we all needed to get back to the basics as human beings.

When I returned to the United States, I launched the Tella-Jerusalem Project. It was named for the tiny village that touched my heart and the city in which I was born in Israel. I used the photographs that I captured while climbing Kilimanjaro and traveling through Tanzania as images on cards that my wife and I sell to raise money for the effort. To date, we have sent thousands of dollars to the Tella Primary School, and we hope to send more. With this money, the school was able to replace its chalk-drawn map with real maps, fix the school's roof, and put doors on the restrooms. Now the children have desks with chairs that were built using the donated money and that bear the name "Tella-Jerusalem" on them.

Dr. Fidelis and I still write to each other. I feel fortunate to have had the opportunity to see Tella, and I will continue to support the Tella Primary School.

The Accidental Cyclist

The intentional cycle of life

Dorothy Stephens

BACK IN THE fall of 1994, my husband and I took a shuttle to Logan airport on our way to visit our daughter Laurie in California. Our driver, a young blond man named Doug, turned out to be a part-time bike tour leader as well as a part-time shuttle driver. He regaled us all the way to the airport with tales of some of the trips organized by Easy Riders, the company he worked for. I was green with envy. I remembered reading a magazine article about a similar trip in Denmark: flat rides through quaint villages by the sea; lunches of mouth-watering Danish cheeses, ham, and crusty bread; delicious dinners served up at charming inns. It had sounded like heaven.

"Oh," I said to Doug, "I've always wanted to do something like that, but it's too late."

"What do you mean, too late?" he asked.

"I'm seventy years old and I haven't been on a bike in fifty years," I said.

"It's not too late," Doug replied. "Just start training right now. You can do it!"

He suggested that I aim for Easy Riders' least challenging tour, six days of cycling on Prince Edward Island in Canada.

When we reached California, I told my daughter about the conversation with Doug. My husband had already said to count him out. In fact, his exact words were, "Are you crazy?"

Laurie was more upbeat. She said, "Mom, go ahead, do it! If you train and get in shape, *I'll* go on a bike trip with you."

When my husband and I got home to Massachusetts, it was winter and snow was on the ground. Biking was the farthest thing from my mind. Then, in February came my seventy-first birthday and a surprise: a new, red 21-speed bicycle. It was the product of long distance conferences between my husband and three children. And hanging on the handlebars was the following message from Laurie:

"When do we leave for Prince Edward Island?"

So then I had to ride. For the first few months that spring, my attempts were pitiful. I wobbled around the empty parking lot at the local yacht club out of breath and my knees turning to jelly. Fifteen minutes was all that I could manage. But I rode all summer, discovered the bike path in town that threads through woods and past ponds and harbor, and by fall, I was riding six or seven miles at a stretch and loving it.

When spring came the following year and the snow melted, I was out on my bike again. Gradually I gained in strength and confidence and rode for long distances. It was then that Laurie and I signed up for the Prince Edward Island tour.

Once on the Island, we rode an average of twenty-five miles per day past green fields and blue ocean, pink sand beaches and red sandstone cliffs, and along quiet country roads bordered by incredible banks of wild flowers. I was hooked. Since then I've been on a number of supported bike trips and have continued to ride as much and as far as I can around my home area north of Boston. I run errands on my bike, ride to the beach for a swim, take my bike on the train to towns twenty or twenty-five miles away, then have a leisurely ride back down the coast toward home. Biking has become my escape and my therapy and has brought moments of joy to my life.

Fast forward to September 2007.

My biking buddy Louise and I have gone for a bike ride along the ocean and have stopped to sit on a bench and eat our sandwiches. A cyclist with a recumbent bike sits on the bench across from us eating his lunch. We begin talking and discussing the pros and cons of recumbent, and I ask if he's ever ridden his on a long trip.

"Not a recumbent," he says. "But I've been on a lot of long bike trips because I'm a bike tour guide."

He tells us that he works for Bike Riders of Boston, and that leads to a discussion of the different companies we've all traveled with. When I mention Easy Riders, he says, "Oh, I worked for them for about six years."

I look at him more closely. He has gray hair but a youthful face and a strong, muscular build to go with his friendly smile.

"Were you also a driver for North Shore Shuttle?" I ask.

"Yeah, I was. Still fill in for them sometimes."

"Is your name Doug?" I ask.

"Yes it is." He looks surprised.

"You're the one who got me into biking!" I tell him the story of how he had encouraged and inspired me, and Laurie too, who began riding regularly after our PEI tour and is now a bike tour guide herself.

Doug shakes his head in amazement. "I *love* stories like that!" he says.

By now we have finished our lunch and I hand him two of my peanut butter oatmeal cookies.

"Thank you!" I say. "Thank you for changing my life."

Lose Your Mind

Sometimes you have to lose your mind
to find your heart

Joseph Civitella

MAURICE WAS A young, ruthless, intellectual wizard who rose through the ranks of the company hierarchy in record time. As a colleague told him, "You're single. You have money. You're good-looking. And you have women. What else do you want from life?" But he also had a softer side, which he kept well hidden, and he nurtured a dream that he told no one about.

One day he heard that Jennifer, the stunning young nurse whom he had met a few weeks earlier, was back on the dating scene. It took him only two days to hook up with her, and they arranged to meet for dinner one evening after her hospital shift.

After he had arrived in the main lobby to pick her up, he learned that she was detained by a last-minute emergency in her ward. He located a newsstand, bought a financial paper, and sat in an empty seat. Close to him was a little boy in a wheelchair, drawing on a pad of paper. Beside the child sat a reserved-looking woman.

After a while he heard the little boy say, "Do you like my drawing?" Maurice looked up. The drawing wasn't very good, and he couldn't quite tell what the child was drawing, but something about it held his attention.

In a flash of long-lost memory, he saw an image of something he had drawn when he himself was young. He also felt an instant pang of sadness, because his parents had thrown it away in disgust, telling him to focus on "serious things." He instantly knew that he couldn't assault the little boy's feelings with the same cold response. Maurice smiled. "Yes, I like it. What is it you're drawing?"

"Stuff I like," replied the little boy. "Sometimes I make it up."

"I see," said Maurice. "You must have a pretty good imagination."

The woman smiled. "Yes, he does," she said.

"My mommy said that I'm pretty good," volunteered the child.

"I agree," said Maurice. "You are pretty good."

"I'm sorry that he bothered you," offered the woman.

"Oh, not a problem," replied Maurice. "His drawing reminded me of something I once drew."

"Are you an artist?" asked the woman.

"No, far from it!" Maurice felt that pang of sadness again.

"Do you want to draw with me?" asked the little boy.

"I'm not very good at all," answered Maurice.

"No, Davey. Let the man do his work," insisted the woman.

Just then Maurice's cellular phone rang. It was Jennifer, informing him that she would be delayed for some time due

to the emergency. He turned once more to the little boy. "Do
you want to be an artist when you grow up?"

"Yes," asserted Davey. "My room at home is filled with
things I drawed."

"Things you drew," corrected the woman.

"It must be a nice room you have." Maurice looked at the
woman, who quickly averted her eyes.

"It is!" exclaimed Davey. "I call it my art house."

"He actually does," said the woman. "One day soon I'm
afraid he'll start charging for admission."

Maurice laughed. "You must take him to quite a few art
galleries, I imagine."

"I used to," replied the woman. "But since my husband
passed away, we haven't been getting out much."

"Oh, I'm sorry."

"That's okay," she said. "Davey's also been having a rough
time with his kidneys."

"What's wrong, if you don't mind me asking?"

"Renal failure," answered the woman. "We're waiting for
a kidney transplant."

Maurice looked at the little boy, who glanced up briefly
with a look of utter innocence in his eyes.

"It doesn't hurt," said Davey as he continued drawing.

Maurice felt a mix of emotions. He wanted to hug the
child and simultaneously punch out at the world. He looked
at the woman.

"What are the chances of him getting one?"

"The doctors tell us that we have to be patient. He's only
six years old, so it can't be just any kidney donor."

Maurice nodded. "And he has to stay in a hospital…"

"He's under observation."

The conversation continued, and then Maurice's cellular phone rang again. He hung up and said, "Well, my evening is free now."

The woman averted her gaze while the boy kept drawing.

"Would you like to get some coffee, or tea, or hot chocolate?" Maurice asked.

Davey looked up immediately. "Can I get a hot chocolate with marshmallows in it?"

"Davey!" The woman shook her head at the child.

"Of course you can," answered Maurice.

"But you probably have more important things to do," suggested the woman.

Maurice felt something stirring inside, and he knew what it was—the sudden longing to share his dream with someone. He gazed into the little boy's innocent eyes and made an instant decision. "Yes," he said, "I did have more important things to do, but somehow they don't seem all that important now." He paused. "In fact, I'd like to tell you about a dream I have."

"Dream?" asked the woman.

"I know," said Maurice. "We don't even know each other."

"You have a secret?" asked Davey.

Maurice smiled and whispered, "Yes, Davey, a secret."

He looked at the woman again and extended his hand. "My name is Maurice."

She hesitated for a moment and then shook his hand in return. "My name is Linda."

"Now, how about that coffee?"

"And a hot chocolate for me!" reminded Davey.

"And a hot chocolate for you," agreed Maurice.

They went to the hospital cafeteria, where Maurice shared his dream with them—to open a free community art gallery that doubled as a café. It would be a place where artists could come in and set up an easel and paint while other patrons looked on. The artists' pieces would then be displayed for sale.

It wasn't exactly the kind of evening Maurice thought he would have, but in many ways it was much more meaningful than expected, and it positively changed the course of his life. It took him three years afterwards to plan his strategy and execute it, and although it was still against sound rational judgment, he let his heart lead him. He left the corporate world to open his art gallery.

Maurice also accomplished something else very significant—he married Linda. And he proudly accepted Davey as his new son.

The name Maurice chose for his art gallery was probably the easiest choice of all. He named it Davey's Art House. The first picture that he proudly framed and hung up was the drawing that Davey had shown him the day they had met at the hospital.

Below the drawing, Maurice placed a plaque stamped with the following words: "Sometimes you have to lose your mind to find your heart." Those words had become his mantra, and they summarized what he had learned from the two most wonderful people whom he met one evening when he wasn't expecting the unexpected.

A Moment of Humility

How a setback became a step up

Elizabeth Anne Hill

As told by Rita Kaye Davis

THE SPRING OF 1999 should have been the best time of my life. Instead, it became a time of great turmoil and necessary change.

On the outside I was an attractive, outgoing, professional thirty-seven-year-old woman with an active social life. My friends and family saw me as adventurous, athletic, and ambitious. On the inside, however, I was lonely and fearful. I felt isolated and misunderstood, as though I didn't belong anywhere. I secretly sensed that I was not good enough and that I would never live up to other people's expectations.

Not surprisingly, I turned to alcohol for solace. Every event in my life was planned around drinking. I was a civilian worker on a military base in Germany, and this setting provided the opportunity to further my addiction. Germans love their beer, and to make matters worse, the entire social structure of the military revolves around drinking. Every day after work I would go to the officers' club or the enlisted club and have cocktails with my co-workers.

Men loved me because I could match them drink for drink. Women loved me because I was the life of the party.

37

But my behavior was a mask to cover up my insecurities. Drinking became my means of fitting in with the crowd.

I received my first DUI in Germany. Then I had two more in Tennessee years later. The consequences were severe. I lost my license and had to rely on other people for everything. But somehow I managed to avoid facing my biggest fear—going to jail.

I received my fourth and final DUI on March 7, 1999, after driving in a complete blackout and nearly hitting an ambulance. The EMS driver alerted the police, who promptly put out an APB on me. They caught up with me just two miles from home. I failed the field sobriety test.

To add to the humiliation, the arresting officers were part of a special unit that filmed DUI arrests. I became the star of my own personal "Cops" episode. As I sat shivering and handcuffed in the back seat of the patrol car, I prayed silently, "God, please help me."

One would think that my fourth DUI arrest would be like a giant red flag waving in my face. Oddly, I never thought that I abused alcohol, and no one else accused me of such abuse, until I met Charles, that is. In retrospect, I could see that I got the help I needed, just not in the form I expected.

"Rita, you have a serious problem," he told me. Charles was appointed as my lawyer, and his words hit me hard. I also knew deep down that he was right.

As this sickening idea sunk in further, we discussed the possibility of going to trial.

"On the positive side," he said, "you're very presentable. But on the negative side, your film debut as 'wrecked Rita' won't do you any favors." At that moment I knew that I had no other choice than to completely surrender. And so I decided to trust Charles to help me make the right decisions. At his urging, I began attending AA meetings, not only because of the support I would receive but also because he thought it would look good in court.

When I arrived at the first AA meeting, I had the familiar feeling of not fitting in. I was overdressed and looked like I had walked into the wrong room. However, it didn't take long for me to feel welcome and at home. The people were warm and friendly, and they wanted nothing more than to share their stories of strength and hope.

At the time, I thought that I had already hit rock bottom when I nearly swerved into an ambulance and then got filmed failing a sobriety test two miles from home. But I was wrong. My lawyer informed me that the best plea bargain I could get was a first offense and six months in jail with the possibility of work release.

I was terrified of going to jail. I asked a friend, "What should I do?"

"This too shall pass," she replied calmly.

Something about that answer resonated with me. I felt as though an angel was whispering in my ear, "God never gives you anything you cannot handle." I decided to accept the jail time.

On September 9, 1999, I faced my greatest fear and entered the Knox County Medium Security Detention Facility in Knoxville, Tennessee, where I began serving my six-month sentence. It was a moment of great humility that changed my life forever.

The first question the other inmates asked me was, "What is someone like you doing here?"

Once again, I felt out of place, and although I felt uncomfortable, I looked at them confidently and said, "Drugs and alcohol do not discriminate."

I was surprised to find that I was treated with kindness and compassion by the guards and other inmates. Everyone there had different stories with varying degrees of dysfunction and crisis in their lives. But I saw that they were all people like me, who were working through their problems and trying to discover who they really were.

While in jail, I faced myself squarely and took responsibility for my actions. As soon as I accepted the fact that I had an addiction, it set my healing into motion. I recognized the earth angels who had been there to guide me on my journey: The bail bondsman who gave me his lawyer's number; my lawyer, Charles, who told me I had a problem and introduced me to AA; my sister Kim and friend Esta, who went with me to court; and John and JoAnn Hohenberg, a well-known and respected Knoxville couple, who allowed me to live with them while out on work release.

I realized that I was in jail not only to face my addiction and allow myself to receive help but also to be a role model for the other inmates. I discovered a profound sense of inner strength and purpose, and I was able to spread a message of hope and perseverance to everyone around me. I even subsequently conducted AA meetings for a year at the jail where I had been incarcerated.

What began as my worst nightmare—a terrifying experience to say the least—turned into an inner quest to find the real me—a life-changing journey from addiction to wholeness. In the end, I recognized that my purpose was simply to live my life joyfully, gratefully, and authentically in the service of others. It was another moment of humility in which I found the greatness in me.

The Carpenter

Getting what you want from the universe

Barbara Elisse Najar

ACCORDING TO MY Assyrian heritage, the name *Najar* means "carpenter." My father's name was Najar, and he was a carpenter of sorts—not by trade but simply because he could make or fix anything. Not surprisingly, that skill has always held great appeal for me; I have always been attracted to a man who is good with his hands.

In late 2005, I ended a love affair that was heading south. As a result, I found myself moving back to a house I had been renting out. My decision to move back home was also fortuitous for my ninety-four-year-old father, who was no longer able to care for himself and asked if he could live with me. I was thrilled that we would become housemates. Living with Dad had its share of stresses because of his failing health, but we relished our time together and created many wonderful memories. It was a great blessing for us both. He died in May 2007 with the words "thank you, thank you!" on his lips. Although he had suffered many losses in his life, such as the premature deaths of my brother and sister, he treasured me and told me so every day.

I had gotten used to having Dad here, and six weeks after his death, I realized I wanted a housemate. So one sunny June morning, I sat down and thought about what I was looking for. I needed someone who was kind, helpful, easygoing, a music lover, spiritually inclined, and felt pride about his or her surroundings. Basically, I needed someone like my Dad. I didn't write all of those attributes in the ad. The ad simply read, "Beautiful townhouse basement efficiency. Lots of light, fireplace." But I kept my real wish list handy. I regarded it as a prayer that the universe was in the process of answering. For years this was how I'd attracted many things to my life, and I believed in its power.

In prior ads for housemates, I had always written "female only." But as I completed the ad, I realized immediately that I wanted to leave the gender open. So this time I did not specify male or female.

I placed the ad and returned to my morning meditation. As I finished, a strong desire surged within me, and I knew that I was ready to meet my life partner. I pulled out my "Ideal Mate" wish list and read it over. It was then that I remembered a technique I'd just learned from my spiritual coach, Barbara. She said that if you want something, simply command the universe to deliver it. So I stood up, pointed my finger to the ground, and shouted in my most commanding voice, "Bring my life partner to me and bring him NOW!!" I felt a sudden rush of energy and smiled. I remember thinking how good that felt! Mind you, I did not connect the newspaper ad with the command I'd just issued. The universe apparently had other ideas.

Four hours later the phone rang. I didn't recognize the name on the caller ID, but then it occurred to me that the ad must have been posted on the Internet by now. When I picked up the phone, a man's voice said, "Hi, my name is Daniel. I'm calling about the ad for your efficiency!" His voice sounded strangely familiar, but I did not know who he was.

That evening I showed the place to an older woman. She was depressed because of the recent loss of her husband, and I knew that she was not a good match for me.

Daniel showed up after the woman had left and could barely wait to get through the door. We sat at my dining room table and discussed what each of us was seeking. We connected immediately. He was six years younger than I and had been on a spiritual path for much of his adult life. Like me, he had also lived in India; he adored animals; he was kind. He was an athlete—a competitive cyclist as well as a runner and a hiker; he was also lean, muscular, and handsome. When I showed him the efficiency, he noticed my cross-country skis under the stairwell and asked if I skied. "I love to cross-country ski, and I've always wanted to do it while camping out," I replied. He just looked at me and shook his head in disbelief.

The longer we talked the more that we found in common with each other. We liked cooking, traveling, and reading; we were introverts and artists of one sort or another. Like my Dad, Daniel was also a superb photographer, which I greatly admired. He loved all kinds of music (something that was very important to me), from classical to country to bluegrass, blues, opera, rock—he liked it all.

There was obviously some strong energy at work here. I took his application and in the following week performed due diligence before deciding to accept him as my new housemate. He was everything I was seeking in a roommate and more. The day before he moved in, he asked if we could go running together. Because of my knee injury (from running), we went swimming instead and began getting to know each other on a deeper level. Despite the strong attraction, and probably because of it, we agreed to postpone becoming physically intimate. We needed to get our bearings.

The year before I met Daniel, a psychic consultant told me that my father was trying to find a partner for me. (I think my father had become impatient with my selection process!) Dad certainly hadn't wasted any time. Not only was Daniel a carpenter, he was the only man I ever dated who used toothpicks—something my father was known for as well. The first week he was here, I found toothpicks everywhere. I realized they were my father's calling cards.

My therapist had long encouraged me to create a loving, nurturing home for myself before trying to partner with someone else. "Once you have settled squarely in your own life, your partner will find you, and he will fit in easily," she assured me.

My *thin thread* was my impulsive decision to keep the gender of my future housemate open and to command the universe to bring my partner to me *now*!

I feel as though I got a "two-for-one deal" from the universe. Living with Daniel is one of the easiest things I've ever done. We mesh perfectly; we are soul mates and still shake our heads in awe at our relationship. He feels deeply connected to my father, whose energy permeates our relationship. Along with that, everything in my house is fixed!

Something else makes me grin. On my mate wish list, I had written squarely, "Will not have to travel to find him." I certainly don't; he's just a short trip downstairs!

Reach Out Before It's Too Late

Friendships are investments
worth making

Leslie Galliker

"**I**F YOU WANT to see Maureen again, then you have to come to Syracuse, tonight." I listened to the words that my friend Jean spoke to me between choking sobs over the phone. I didn't believe what I was hearing. Maureen, a member of our trio since first grade, was dying.

I walked slowly down the hallway at the hospital where I worked. X-ray techs hurried past me, busy with their portables and films. I had so many issues to deal with that night—there were computer problems to tend to, dictation to transcribe from mumbling doctors, and four more hours to put in at work. My mind whirled. I thought to myself, "This can't be." Maureen was not much older than fifty. Other thoughts pushed their way into the mix—my recently dissolved marriage and discontent with my job to name two. Then a jarring thought erased all the others. I had not seen or spoken to Maureen in a few years. How could that be? Forgetfulness and a hectic schedule on Maureen's part but anger and ego-trip on my part. Why should I be the one to always write and call? Especially when I don't get a response! Regardless of whose fault it was, we hadn't been in touch for a long time.

Call it conscience or God whispering in my ear, but all I could think of at that moment was this was my first best friend. We had known each other through thick and thin for almost half a century, and now she was dying hundreds of miles away. It was almost Labor Day, and I decided that I would labor no more. I hastily scribbled a note to my supervisor. Would I still have a job when I returned, I wondered. I ran out of the hospital and turned my car in the direction of Princeton Junction. I would catch the train to New York's Pennsylvania Station, and from there another train to Syracuse. I could then hail a taxi to take me to the hospital.

I was extremely tense the entire way to Penn Station. When I found the right train, I barely noticed the other passengers. I was jostled both before and after finding a seat, a man snored to beat the band, a drunken lady in great need of a shower continually bumped her head against my shoulder, and a baby whimpered louder and louder. They all became a blur. I closed my eyes for a minute and began to believe that I had just had a nightmare. Then I opened my eyes, realized where I was and why, and knew that this was all too real. I was going to see one of my best friends who was dying of intestinal cancer and most likely had less than a day left to live.

Images raced through my brain: Maureen and I at Alex's Soda Shop, sipping milkshakes at a table crowded with some other friends. Her mother worked there, and we would go back to Maureen's apartment, where my mother picked me up when she finished work. I had fun at that apartment. Rex,

Maureen's caramel-colored cocker spaniel, greeted me with a gruff woof. Maureen's Nana puttered in one of the tiny apartment rooms, softly singing an Irish ditty from her childhood. I remembered the chill of the car rides on our trips to visit her many relatives in Scranton and Syracuse. We had to head out at dawn—Maureen's mother insisted. So Maureen and I bundled up in the back seat, giggling even at that early hour, but before long we went back to sleep. My memories jumped to many years later, when I was a bridesmaid at Maureen and Lee's wedding. They had some problems over the years, but I knew that Lee loved her and that he must be devastated by Maureen's condition.

God must have been with me that night—I am usually awful with directions, but I made it to the station with no major problems. I had just arrived when I saw the listings for trains to upstate New York. As luck might have it, the train track I had to find was very close by. The lights dimmed once I was aboard, but I didn't sleep. I recalled what I had last heard from Jean about Maureen's life, which unfolded so far from where we grew up in Manhattan. She was an executive, Jean told me, who loved her job but hated the traveling that it required. She had children who were now adults. I remembered all the mischief that frayed our nerves when our kids would get together on my visits to Camp LeJeune, where Maureen and her family lived on base. Maureen would soon be a first-time grandmother. I cried when I realized that she most likely would not see her first grandchild. Maureen had a vibrant life, and it was painful to think about it coming to an end.

The train ride to Syracuse seemed surprisingly short. Maybe the numerous wonderful, sad, funny, and painful moments that I was recalling of our long friendship made the trip seem shorter. I remember the tremendous sense of gratitude I felt when the cabbie outside the Syracuse train station said, yes, I could give him a certain amount of cash and put the rest of the fare on my credit card. I almost whimpered with happiness, as I had not even thought about money when I dashed out of the hospital.

Before long, I arrived in Maureen's room. Jean sat by her bed and held one of her hands. Lee had a blank expression on his face. Maureen had always been pale, but now she was ghostly white. I could see that her beautiful blue eyes were open, but not aware. A nurse entered the room and gave Maureen pain medication. She responded with a growl, the only angry sound Maureen could make with a tube down her throat. I bent down and whispered in her ear. I told Maureen, "I love you." I counted her rapidly slowing breaths. She slept a few minutes, so Jean and I decided we would get something to eat. We were gone for no more than ten minutes. When we came back into her room, doctors and nurses were leaning over her bed and tubes were being removed. Lee stood in a corner, his body shaking, silently sobbing. Maureen had not wanted her friends to see her take that last breath.

A few years later, my pain still seems fresh. Yet Maureen must be smiling, because she knew how impatient I could get when things didn't go my way. Soon after I got back to New Jersey, I left my job at the hospital for a daytime job. I began to call the friends I had meant to get in touch with "some day." Where wounds had to be healed, I swallowed my pride and took the first step. Best of all, Jean and I see each other regularly in Manhattan. After losing Maureen I realized the importance of reaching out before it is too late.

Angel Within the Wreckage

Unexpected miracles do happen

Leslie Martini

THE HOUSE SAT high in the mountains, where jagged, snow-covered peaks revealed breathtaking backdrops with traces of sunlight peering above their highest points. From the window, I watched clumpy white snowflakes fall on the driveway and cover every inch of the car's black hood. Immune to the four-hour drive back to Boston, I lingered idly in the kitchen. My mind shifted gears between the threatening weather brewing outside and the tranquil state of the sleeping newborn in my arms. This was the baby my friend Sandy had waited for. After years of infertility, she finally had her child. The baby was a gift and a gentle reminder that unexpected miracles do happen. By the time I said my final goodbyes and made my way outside, the blackness of the car had been transformed to white.

The temperature gauge inside the car rose ever so slowly to ten degrees as I made my way down into the valley. Although it was midday, the sun had dipped behind the mountains, making way for heavy, gray clouds. Moments later, the valley was a winter wonderland, with snow blanketing the black pavement before my eyes as I accelerated onto Highway 89 just south of Stowe, Vermont.

A care package of fresh salsas and chocolate sauces from Sandy occupied the passenger seat next to me. Along with the package sat my unfinished Christmas cards, which I had meant to work on while Sandy and the baby napped. I thought about the number of journeys that those unfinished cards had made in the last few weeks. The cards traveled many miles only to remain on the passenger seat just days before Christmas. The mere sight of them evoked not holiday spirit but anxiety. This year the pictures were taken early. Both of my daughters cooperated and were pleased to do their part in jumpstarting the holiday season. This was to be the year when the cards were assembled during Thanksgiving break and checked off the list by December 1. Now, weeks later, the remaining steps of assembling the cards and mailing them had become less of a priority.

The sound of my homemade CD skipping shook me from my holiday daydreams and brought my attention back to the road ahead, where snow was accumulating quickly. I engaged in a tug of war with my seat belt as I reached for the fast-forward button on the CD player. The seat belt's grip felt reassuring. A tingling sensation in my left hand was an alarm, calling to my attention the whiteness of my knuckles. I loosened my grip and felt the sweat in my palm, sticky on the leather steering wheel. A deep breath and few wrist bends restored the color to my hand and allowed my shoulders to recover too. All of my body parts seemed to be speaking at once, calling for relaxation.

My eyes were fixated on the intervals of dusty white highway and the tiny specks of black pavement that were now becoming an anomaly. Although my body had long sensed the changing road conditions, my mind was slow to follow. I turned up the volume on track 8, a version of Pearl Jam's "Last Kiss." I pondered the lyrics, "the sound of the crash that night . . . Oh where oh where did my baby go . . ."

I don't recall the decision to hit the brake, but my reflexes must have taken over. The sensation of spinning out of control is what I remember. The car that I was driving proved no match for the black ice, and I slid full speed off Highway 89. My fears of death overtook me momentarily, and the thoughts of children without a mother gripped me. I vividly remember the peaceful feeling of being transported elsewhere. I felt nothing as the car rolled over, my head smashed into the roof, the windows shattered, and the car slammed against the ground in a gully out of sight. Lying there in the stillness, I lost consciousness, peacefully dreaming of my children.

Then the angel came. He appeared to me as though in a dream. He was an off-duty EMT who happened to be driving on the opposite side of the highway. He saw the accident from the onset, reporting on the number of times the car rolled before disappearing from the road. By the time he'd exited the highway and turned around, my body was in a snowbank, half frozen. I heard him before I saw him. His voice was detailing my estimated weight and height to someone on the phone.

I could hear faint music from his car stereo, playing the words, "oh where oh where did my baby go . . ."

His face was tender and white like the snow around him. I must have been half-conscious because he seemed to appear and then disappear. He was trying to talk to me, but I was so tired. I wanted to talk to him and tell him about my children and what they looked like. As I slipped in and out of consciousness, I managed to form the words that I longed to share, telling him over and over about my children needing a mother. I needed to get to them. He unclenched my frozen, bleeding hand and removed from it a picture of my girls.

Blinding lights were shining down on me, rudely waking me from the faraway place to where I had been transported. I opened and closed my eyes, fighting to get back to that quiet world and away from this current place of sterile walls and unrelenting beeping sounds. My body seemed to belong to someone else as I remained frozen against the cold metal table to which I was strapped. Tears formed in my eyes as I tried to put the pieces together, my head pounding from the effort. I reached up, trying to find the pain, feeling the tears mixing with the blood oozing from the bandages. I asked for my husband and then for the man who brought me here, but no one answered. I wanted to thank the angel. The room was silent.

There were seven more accidents after mine, but none were as serious. Eventually, that section of Highway 89 where I crashed was closed. The talk in the hospital was that it had been a miracle that I survived. The head trauma and concussion were the worst part, and the effects of those injuries plagued me for years. The physical evidence lay splattered across the highway in the form of salsa and chocolate sauces, shattered containers, the contents of my purse, and the unfinished holiday cards and pictures.

The angel was never found. But I know that he existed. He saved my life and then went on to do other work that angels do. He knew that my children needed their mother, and he knew that he could bring me back to them. I believe in angels and in miracles. Both came to me that day on the side of the road. Both are with me now, gently reminding me how close I was to teetering off the *thin thread* that distinguishes life from death—the thread that keeps us from faltering.

Fast Food for Thought

When you're "here,"
and you really hear

Laura College

MOST PEOPLE LIVE their lives by taking whatever path seems easiest at the moment a decision is required. Whether subconsciously or purposefully, they are drawn to the simplest solutions, the straightest edge, or the widest berth. They are as deaf to the knock of opportunity as a dictator who turns a blind eye to the cries of his people.

I grew up in a home where conformity was expected. My parents paid their bills, went to work, helped me with my homework, and disciplined me when I was wrong. I essentially was raised in the epitome of the American dream, and although I would later come to realize that this wasn't the journey I wanted to embark on, it was a safe and loving environment, for which I will always be grateful.

Nevertheless, I began to stray from that environment when I was in my late teens. By the time I reached the ripe old age of twenty-one, I'd pretty much decided that I was the black sheep of my family.

Unsure of my future and blinded by conflict between what I could have and what I really wanted, I took a job as shift leader at a local fast food restaurant. It was a steady paycheck, something to do, and a safe harbor in which I could rest my sails while I contemplated my purpose in life.

I knew that the world was full of many possibilities that appealed intensely to me, but I wasn't sure how I might take advantage of those opportunities at such a young age. I had no college education, no skills, no prospects; I was lost in a sea of opportunity that had yet to solidify into anything I could use constructively.

While working at the fast food restaurant, I met the man who would one day become my husband. He was my soul mate, a man trapped in the same holding pattern in which I'd floundered for the better part of my life. He was flipping burgers when he could have been starting his own dot.com corporation, performing surgery, or arguing case law in court. We connected without making any effort to connect.

During most weeks, he and I worked the graveyard shift. It was just the two of us in a darkened fast food joint, working the drive-thru when there were customers and playing cards when there weren't. We discussed our hopes, our dreams, our passions, and our fears. It was to him that I finally made the admission that would later change my life.

"I want to be a writer," I told him, nervously shuffling a deck of cards and hoping that he wouldn't laugh in my face.

"Then you should be a writer," he blurted without a trace of guile.

He was right, of course, but I wasn't ready to decide whether writing was the best path for me, so I nodded agreeably and dealt the cards.

Two weeks later we again worked the graveyard shift, growing increasingly grainy-eyed and stiff-muscled as the night wore on. At two o'clock on that Sunday morning, the after-last-call bar rush began, and the drive-thru soon was filled with drunken college kids.

My future husband fired up the grill, and I began taking orders through my drive-thru headset. The words, "Can I take your order please?" seemed to resonate in my skull with the intensity and irritation of nails on a chalkboard. When I opened the window for the umpteenth time to collect money and pass drinks into the hands of thirsty customers, I was sure that I was going to throw a bucket of fryer grease in the face of the next person who ordered a "jumbo burger, hold the onions."

The customer outside my window was on his cell phone, talking rapidly with a Bluetooth device firmly attached to his ear. As I took his fifty-dollar bill and handed him a medium Diet Coke, I heard him say, "Bill I've been telling you for years, you'll never make any real money working for someone else."

Usually, the private conversations of customers in the drive-thru line were like the steady din of excited conversation before the opening number at a rock concert. I rarely distinguished one word from the next, but this customer's words reached my ears.

"What did you say?" I asked.

The customer, who was dressed in a fine blue suit, said, "Oh, I'm sorry, I was talking on the phone."

"I know," I mumbled and then suddenly ripped the drive-thru headset off my head, snagging a tangle of hair in the earpiece but not noticing the sting of pain that followed. I handed the customer back his fifty-dollar bill.

"Tonight it's on the house."

From the grill, my husband-to-be announced that the next order was ready, so I bagged it and handed it through the window. "You should feel honored," I told the customer. "You get the last fast-food burger I'll ever serve in this hell-hole. I owe it all to you." Before he could reply, I shut the window and latched it closed. I unclipped the drive-thru belt from around my waist and headed back to the grill.

"There's a line all the way out to the street!" my future husband said incredulously.

"Guess they'll have to find somewhere else to stave off their hangovers," I replied.

We finished the prep work for the following day, cleaned the grill, mopped the floors, and punched out without calling anyone. I used my Shift Leader keys to lock the doors from inside, and left a note for my boss saying we wouldn't be back. Then we got in my car and parked across the street to watch the customers we despised with such vehemence pounding on the drive-thru window.

The next day, armed with as much passion and determination as talent, my future husband and I started a ghostwriting business. Over the subsequent months, it flourished and floundered, rose and fell, ebbed and flowed, but we never regretted the decision to leave the main river for the far more satisfying tributaries along its side. I wrote stories, articles, and brochures, and he handled the business end of the venture. Before long, we were poised to take the next great leap in our adventure.

Sometimes the easiest path is the right one, but you can find greater excitement and pleasure on the roads less traveled. Take a moment in your safe harbor to regroup and to narrow your desires. But don't stay too long, because you might get stuck on "Main Street."

Orphans, Best Friends, Sisters

The power of dreams

Ana Barlow

"ANA?" HER VOICE quivered as she said my name. It was gentle and familiar, and I realized how much I had missed her. There was igniting joy in her eyes when she learned that the American family that adopted me had now come to adopt her. A surge of love and happiness rushed through my veins. After two years of separation, we reunited under a new name—a name that made us sisters.

Any orphan was glad to be adopted, even though little information was disclosed to the child other than the fact that a family was coming for him or her. It was a celebrated occasion in the orphanage, and no questions were raised about the future happiness of an adoptee. Tania's adoption was a planned surprise. She had no idea that I would be part of the family adopting her.

We grew up together, hoping and praying that the orphanage would not be the only home we knew. My prayer had been answered, and Tania's prayers would be answered as well.

Traveling back to Russia made me realize how distant my former home had become. I was going back to visit what was still so much a part of my life, hoping to find everything the same or better. Yet I was deeply burdened by the state of life that was my own not long before.

Bleakness and destitution echoed through the entrance of orphanage number 3. It hung oppressively as I walked up the mud-tracked stairs and through the main entry to group number 6. The paint on the walls was peeling. The outdated, dirty, and forsaken surroundings contrasted with more recent memories of cheery windows and fairytale murals. It was hard to believe that two years earlier I had been one of the eighteen children in group number 6 in orphanage number 3. I felt sad and confused and did not know where to find rest in this place that was once my home.

I struggled to find some connections that would remove this horrible feeling that I was a stranger here. We had spent hours playing dolls together and endlessly chattering about our future. I remember one time in particular when we made a promise to each other to "sign papers" when we were grown up that would make us official sisters. There was nothing whimsical to us about the idea—anything was possible out in the big world. As soon as we were old enough to leave the orphanage, we would live together in an apartment and have all the things that normal people who weren't raised in an orphanage had. Our adoption into the same family was beyond anything we could ever imagine.

Standing there, with tear-stained faces, we were overjoyed to be together again. Even now as I reflect on the experience, everything that happened to me before she became my sister seems a blur; I can't imagine life without her. They say that every person has a dream, a fantasy that follows them through life. Although my dream has become a reality, I often find myself spellbound by its unveiling. My adoptive parents, without my prompting, came to love one girl among a hundred, and they made this girl, who happened to be my best friend, my sister. Later, holding my sister's hand, I recalled the following proverb: "Save a life, and you save the world." My parents did not just save two lives; they saved the world twice over.

Safe Landing

*The true essence of kindness
that saved my daughter's life*

Peter Victor

SIT IN MY seat sipping a beer. My fourteen-month-old
daughter, Susie, sleeps peacefully in my lap. The clouds
and blue sky zipping by outside our window provide a pleasant backdrop for our flight from Hartford, Connecticut, to
Oakland, California. Susie and I are making the flight alone
after my wife Margaret and son Rocky had taken the train.
We are traveling across the country for a family reunion in
sunny Oakland.

I order my second beer, settle deeper into my seat, and
turn my attention to the novel that sits neglected on my lap.
As I read the first page, a child's groan brings my attention
back to my daughter. She is obviously waking and looks uncomfortable. She felt a little warm earlier, and I thought it
was remnants of a cold that she has been fighting for the past
several days. I flip up my tray and prepare to begin pacing the
aisle with Susie. Walking with Susie in my arms always settles
us both into a feeling of deep contentment.

But as I stand and move toward the aisle, Susie's moans
suddenly become shrieks. She begins to twist violently in my
arms, her face contorted and her body stiff. I look down and

wrap one arm around her and frantically press the stewardess's call button. A chime sounds between Susie's shrieks.
The book I have been reading is kicked into the aisle while
I desperately try to keep hold of Susie. Suddenly I hear a
woman's voice above the din; "My name is Peggy Moyers.
I'm a pediatric intensive care nurse from Texas. Do you need
help with that child?"

I turn and see a large woman behind me with her eyes
locked on Susie. Things are moving quickly as Susie begins
convulsing violently. I let Peggy hold Susie. Peggy begins
walking quickly to First Class. I follow, feeling helpless and
wondering if my child is dying.

Peggy clears two seats and positions them in the reclined
position. She quickly strips Susie to her diaper. The stewardess
brings in a stethoscope as Peggy struggles to keep Susie down
while listening for vital signs. A group of first-class passengers
joins me as we all watch Peggy tend to my baby girl. "Do you
need anything else?" the stewardess asks.

Peggy answers without looking up, "Yes, land this plane
in the closest big city with a really good hospital." The stewardess recoils; she had been expecting a request for water or
napkins. She hurries out and heads to the cockpit. She returns,
looking pale.

"We're going to Denver," she says.

I glance from Susie to the window. I can see the distant airport looming ahead. It looks as though we are free-falling from
the clouds to the airport. As I nervously watch our approach
to the airport, I hear Susie's crying and Peggy's calming words.
The plane jolts us as the wheels hit the tarmac. The whistling

of the wind and the brakes join Susie's cries to form one loud wail. The plane turns, and I look through the window again to see the blinking red lights of an ambulance on the runway.

I watch as airport workers wheel a gangway up to the plane. A loud mechanical sound fills the front end of the plane and then I feel a blast of fresh cold air as the front door of the plane opens. Two paramedics enter the plane carrying a stretcher. One turns to me. "Are you the girl's father?" I nod. The paramedic turns back to Susie and speaks to me again. "Get what you need, but make it fast. We're leaving now." I follow them and climb into the back of an ambulance. I hear the siren wail as we begin speeding away. I look out the back window of the ambulance and see the gangway moving away from the plane as workers position the plane for takeoff. I turn my eyes back to Susie and see her crying. Her face is bathed in perspiration.

The waiting room at the hospital looks sterile. Everything is too quiet. I look at the phone on the wall, and I think about my wife Margaret and our son. I pick up the phone and dial a collect call to my brother-in-law in Oakland. My brother-in-law answers, and I hear his booming voice as he says, "Hey, when are you going to be here?" He senses the urgency as I ask to speak with Margaret.

"What's up, hon?" she says. I try to respond but only manage to say, "Susie . . . plane . . . we're in Denver," and I begin to cry.

The doctor enters the room holding a clipboard. He looks at me and says confidently, "Susie is going to be fine. We believe she has had a febrile seizure. This is a seizure caused by a

8

THIN THREAD STORIES

high temperature. You did say that she has had a cold, right? The only way we can tell for certain is with a spinal tap. But I don't think that's necessary in this case. I just spoke with your wife Margaret, and she's catching a plane from Oakland and will be here early in the morning. By that time, I think we'll feel comfortable releasing Susie. She's awake and asking for you." He smiles and gestures for me to follow.

But when we enter Susie's room, we find her fast asleep. I pull up a chair to her bedside as the doctor leaves the room. I doze off, and when I wake hours later I notice the dim light of early dawn through the window. I glance down at Susie. One arm is strapped down with an IV attached. I begin stroking her forehead and softly singing a song that we often sing together while playing paddy cake. Her eyes flicker and one arm rises above the bed—palm out—she is playing paddy cake. At that moment I know everything is going to be all right.

Margaret is the rock of our family, and by the time she reaches the hospital room, she has arranged for the transfer of the luggage that we left on the plane. She also has booked a flight for two adults and one child from Denver to Oakland, and she has asked about the nurse who had been by Susie's side in her moment of need.

Peggy Moyers was physically and emotionally exhausted from her "vacation." Her class reunion was wonderful, but her thoughts had been with the young girl she had met on the plane. As she walks slowly up her front walk, she hears her front door open. Her husband is looking at her with misty eyes. He steps to the side, and Peggy sees a bouquet of flowers with a card on her kitchen table. She walks in and picks up the card and reads, "Susie is fine and we cannot thank you enough. We will be in touch. Stephen and Margaret."

I glance up from my Editor's desk to look at the photo on the wall. It's a picture of Susie as a high school junior. My eyes linger on the photo as a slow, thankful smile crosses my face. I think of that tender moment in the hospital years ago. That moment has made me realize the infinite value in a young life—how strong, fragile, and important it is. I also now realize that our whole world can change on a Tuesday, Thursday, or any other day. I am now keenly aware of the magic that exists in every situation and how people can "appear" and be present in our greatest moments of need. And I know that Susie and I benefited from this magic on a plane ride years ago.

Ten Questions for the Dalai Lama

Your wish is my command:
applying the law of attraction

Elizabeth Anne Hill

M Y NAME IS Rick Ray. I am a world traveler, writer, and filmmaker. I began my trek around the world over twenty-five years ago and have explored places such as Lebanon, Israel, Syria, Jordan, Burma, Vietnam, Myanmar, and Ethiopia. I have made twelve documentaries about world cultures while studying in detail the environment and traditions of these countries.

I spend so much time abroad that my own country often feels foreign to me. After visiting places like Italy and New Zealand, I wondered why Americans don't get together in the evenings more often to commune over dinner and a glass of wine. I wondered why the poorest places on earth seem to have the most self-sufficient, happy, smiling, and seemingly content people. Why are the rich so stressed out, scattered, and unhappy? Why does monetary wealth not equate to inner wealth?

These were some of the issues that I often pondered. I had no idea, however, that I would get the chance to pose my questions to one of the wisest men in the world until I received an interesting job offer. An American production company wanted to hire me to shoot a commercial film about the wonders of India.

They didn't promise to pay me much money but they did offer a rare opportunity—to meet with and interview the Dalai Lama at his home in Dharamsala, India.

I didn't have to think about the job offer for very long because I have always felt a kinship with the Tibetan leader. When other guys my age were worshipping sports heroes, I was idolizing the Dalai Lama.

Unfortunately, upon arriving in India, I discovered that no one knew anything about the purported interview. I then realized then that I had nearly six months to figure out on my own how I was going to meet the spiritual leader.

India is a mystical place where anything can happen, so I don't know whether it was magic or fate that led me to an eighty-year-old driver named Geeta Ram Ranote. He was quite an interesting character, reminding me of a genie, because for every wish I had he knew a way to make it happen.

"Geeta Ram, can we film at the Taj Mahal at sunset?"

"Yes, sir. I will reserve a space for you."

"Geeta Ram, can we meet the President of India and interview him?"

"No problem, sir."

When I told him that I wished to interview the Dalai Lama, he seemed undaunted by my request and suggested that I write to his Holiness to propose a meeting. I admit that I was quite skeptical about writing a letter, given my understanding of the Indian postal system. Geeta Ram explained that we would not be sending a letter but an email. He just happened to have the Dalai Lama's email address!

I was doubtful once again, but he took me to a cyber cafe and I sent off my request. I had an irrational fear of ending up in the Dalai Lama's spam filtering system, which couldn't be good Karma, but the electronic address Geeta Ram gave me was the Dalai Lama's actual email. Within a few days I received a response, which said that the Dalai Lama was quite busy, but there was an opening in four months' time. I was told that I would be granted ten questions and a forty-five minute interview. I was in utter amazement that I had managed to secure a meeting with the man who is thought to be the reincarnation of the living Buddha. It was obvious that the film producers had not attempted to set up an interview.

As I traveled across India and the Himalaya Mountains, I spent the next ninety days thinking about the questions I would ask. I had decided to immerse myself in Buddhism by living in a Tibetan monastery in the most remote part of India, known as the Nubra Valley. A feeling of extraordinary tranquillity pervaded the entire monastery. I felt as though I was on the rooftop of the world and that somehow I had been transported closer to heaven.

After much contemplation, I finally compiled my list of ten questions. But as the day of the meeting drew near, I began to feel unsure about my questions, so I emailed my friends to see what questions they would ask. They weren't much help. They came up with all kinds of silly suggestions like, "What is Richard Gere's phone number," or the clichéd "What is the meaning of life?"

The Dalai Lama is a very practical man, and I had been warned that he doesn't suffer fools easily. His Holiness likes discussions that meet his own interests as well as the interests of his interviewer. If he senses that someone is there to make a point or is insincere, he will immediately cut the interview short.

Eventually the day of the interview arrived, and I felt the pressure mounting. In addition to wondering whether I had chosen the right ten questions, I wrestled with my nervousness and my camera equipment. If I were rejected after such a long personal journey, it would be the most humiliating moment of my life.

As soon as the Dalai Lama entered the room, however, everything changed. It was a moment I will remember for the rest of my life. He exuded immense love, warmth, and kindness. He was smiling and kidding around. He grabbed the microphone and clipped it on his robe, doing a mock sound check, all the while giggling mischievously. I was immediately put at ease by his infectious laugh.

He turned to me, smiled, and I began the interview. It lasted for over an hour. We talked about philosophy, politics, history, and religion. We talked about nonviolence, truth, faith, and science.

He was so gracious, and the experience was magical. I still do not know how or why I was chosen to interview this great man. I am no one important. But I believe that somehow it was my destiny to make this film and bring the Dalai Lama's timely message of peace to the world.

When I saw the backdrop of the Dalai Lama's life and all that he has been through, it lent much more meaning to his compassion. He claims to be a simple monk, but he has led a life that is anything but simple. For the past forty-nine years he has lived as a refugee from his beloved Tibet because he was driven out by the Chinese waging an ongoing vicious attack on his people and his culture. Yet he expresses no bitterness, only love, kindness, and forgiveness. I could imagine the powerful healing that would take place in the world if other leaders set the same example of patience and wisdom for their own people.

When asked how the experience has affected me, I say that I am trying to live up to the Dalai Lama's belief that if you live your life truthfully you will have nothing to explain, justify, or defend. I believe that he is a spiritual leader with a higher calling. He is able to laugh at himself and at life. He is a man of profound wisdom, practical lessons, and endearing humor. My greatest wish is that his Holiness will someday grant me another ten questions.

Q'ing up for S'More Love

Sometimes Mother
does know best

Kathy Shiels Tully

"A NDY AND I are having a barbecue on July 3, and we'd like you to come," Eileen said.

My best friend Eileen lived with her fiancé, Andy. They occupied the top floor of a two-family house, where Andy had built a large deck off the kitchen. It was perfect for a summer barbeque.

"I can't. My parents are coming up to visit," I replied. It was sad to admit, but every summer my parents would drive up from New York to deliver my air conditioner and then return in the fall to retrieve it. My small condo didn't have much storage space. My mother realized that if they stored it for me, they would have two visits that I couldn't refuse.

"Bring them!" Eileen said.

The thought of bringing my parents to a barbecue made me feel like a child instead of a woman nearing her thirty-fourth birthday. I felt that my single status troubled my mother because she feared that my sister, my two brothers, and I might never marry. My parents had never pushed marriage as the ultimate goal in life. Instead, they'd say, "Just be happy." But as we aged into our thirties, my mother changed her mind.

Her friends were having grandchildren, and I think she felt left out.

One of my sisters had married and had two kids. That took some pressure off us. I had waited this long for the right man, and I'd wait longer if necessary.

Eileen and I then had the first disagreement in our ten-year friendship. "Bring them! I want them to come," Eileen pleaded.

"I'll be the only one at the party with her parents!" I whined.

"No you won't. Renee is bringing her two kids," she laughed.

"What if there's a guy there?" I asked. But I had already met all of Andy's friends when he assumed the role of my personal *yenta*. There was no one left.

When my parents arrived, I laid down the rules. I told them, "You can go, have a beer and a burger, and then leave!" They agreed.

July 3 was a beautiful day. I walked in ahead of my parents, through the kitchen and out onto the deck, where the party was. I scanned the deck for any new men, but I didn't see any.

The smell of burgers and steaks cooking wafted in the air. Eileen had arranged a picnic table with an assortment of summer salads. The crowded deck was perfect for a singles scene, but my parents wanted to sit down. Sitting down on a bench near the table with the salads, I sat between them.

After filling our plates with food, my mother wasted no time.

"What about this one?" she asked, pointing with her eyes to a guy across the deck while she ate her hamburger.

"No," I said.

Seconds later. "What about that one?" She asked, pointing to another man.

"Ma!" I pleaded, "He has a girlfriend sitting right next to him!" She finished her burger in silence and then made one more try.

"What about *that* one?"

"Hmmm...where did he come from?" I mumbled. I had never seen him before. He wasn't my usual slick, corporate type. He was more outdoorsy and rugged—and tall.

"Go talk to him," my mother prodded.

"No!"

Suddenly, my father said, "He seems like a nice guy." Something in his voice touched my heart.

"How would you know?"

He just shrugged and said, "I don't know."

"O-kaaay," I said. "I'll do anything to end this matchmaking game!"

Standing up, I walked toward the grill, where he was standing. I saw a bag of marshmallows on one of the tables, some chocolate bars, and boxes of graham crackers. Using my years of Girl Scout training, I quickly assembled some gooey treats. Turning around, I smiled at him and said, "S'mores?"

I cringed, but the mystery man seemed amused and hungry. Our eyes connected as he reached for the plate, and at that moment I felt as though fairy dust had fallen on us from the heavens. Or was it his sparkling blue eyes that drew me in? It felt as if we were alone on that deck. Right there I knew deep in my soul that he was *the one*.

His name was Joe, and he was a skiing buddy of Andy's. In fact, Andy had invited Joe on a winter ski trip that I went on back in February, but Joe had cancelled at the last minute.

We chatted until some other girl interrupted and began flirting with Joe. Annoyed that he seemed to like her, I returned to my parents' table. They were sitting there like basketball coaches eager to hear the play-by-play.

After relaying the events, I scanned the deck again for him. He'd left! The next day I called Eileen and Andy to say thanks and to investigate.

"What was the name of that skiing friend of yours again?" I queried.

Andy caught on immediately. "Now that I think about it, the two of you would make a perfect couple."

I met Joe again three weeks later after a trip to the beach got cancelled. Eileen said that she and Andy were going hiking with some of his friends in New Hampshire, and she asked if I wanted to go.

I was immediately suspicious. Andy had told me that Joe kept a camp in New Hampshire. I asked, "Is this a fix-up?" Eileen reassured me that it wasn't. When we drove into an old, run-down summer camp, a bearded bear of man ran out and redirected us. "Everyone's staying at Tully's," he told us.

"I knew it! This is a fix-up!" I exclaimed.

When I walked in and saw him and the shocked look in his eyes, I realized that he had no idea I was coming. As the crowd of crunchy granola types mingled, an older woman approached me.

"Hi. What's your name? What do you do? Where do you live?" She asked.

I told her, and then she said, "That's only two miles from my son, Joe." She turned and yelled, "Hey, Joe, come over here." Then she introduced us without realizing that it was a re-introduction.

She looked at me and then she turned and looked at him and said, "I think you should ask her out for drinks." Then she paused. "No, drinks and dinner," she added and then walked away.

The weekend was hectic. I hiked with friends while Joe entertained his relatives. There was such a crowd that we never got to talk.

On Sunday night, he asked for my phone number. I also took his. On Monday night, I sat waiting for the phone to ring because I was certain that he'd call. My stomach knotted. I called Eileen, and she said, "Wait a while. Don't call him and scare him off." But I called anyway.

He sounded surprised but pleased. "I was going to call you but I was just balancing my checkbook." We made a dinner date for that Thursday. After dinner, he kissed me for two hours. I didn't stop smiling for days.

Twelve years and two daughters later, we're both smiling. And every July, we break out the s'mores and celebrate.

A True Military Mission

There is something to gain
from even the greatest losses

Joseph Civitella

ROBERT WAS AN army reservist who worked in intelligence gathering, but he also had trained for front-line combat. In his late twenties, he spent extended periods of time at the military base near his hometown. He consistently demonstrated many good qualities in the performance of his duties and garnered the encouragement of his superiors in charting a promising career path in the military service.

In a few instances, Robert was stationed in war-torn locations but was never involved in direct combat. He said the following prayer when his colleagues left on a mission: "Godspeed my friends and by the good graces of providence may you return unharmed." On most occasions everyone returned to the base safely or with manageable injuries. Every once in a while, troops came back with serious injuries or in body bags.

They all chose army life knowing the risks involved, Robert reminded everyone. The reasons for engaging in combat were often very complex, and many decisions were beyond the control of the troops. It served no useful purpose to be angry or resentful because of what happened on a battlefield.

During a planned layoff at home one day, he received an envelope. When he opened it, he found his new deployment papers; he was going to Afghanistan. He would be stationed at an international compound outside Kabul for a twelve-month term.

"Why Afghanistan?" asked his mother.

"I don't question my orders," answered Robert.

"You could be in harm's way there," she protested.

"I know, Mom," he tried to reassure her, "but I won't be involved in direct combat."

"You'll be in danger, son," added his dad. "The situation there is unsettled, and the enemy is mostly invisible."

"They're mostly invisible until we catch them, Dad," countered Robert, "and that's why I need to go there—to help our troops find them."

Aside from the predictable enigmas of a foreign land, Robert's deployment turned out to be uneventful until one fateful day three months into his tour of duty. He and three armed officers left the compound en route to a region of growing turmoil west of the base. They were to remain at a safe distance from the area of conflict, and Robert was to survey the terrain as best he could with his high-powered binoculars.

He was sitting in the passenger seat of an armored vehicle while one of the officers was driving and two others were seated in the back. Each of them attended to the job at hand, and very few comments were spoken. The last words Robert recalled hearing were uttered by one of the officers in the back seat, "Watch for explosive—"

The blast detonated with deadly force. Robert was ejected from the vehicle and landed yards away. He immediately felt an excruciating pain in his right leg and grabbed his thigh. Blood was everywhere. He screamed, but his agonized yells were drowned out by the sound of the vehicle's gas tank burning uncontrollably. Before passing out, he noticed that there were no other human sounds around him.

Days after the event, Robert lay in a hospital bed staring at the anomaly below his waist. He had only one leg remaining. The rescue team and field doctors had done their best to save his limb, but it was so mangled that amputation was the only feasible option. To add to his chagrin, his worst fears were also confirmed—his three companions had perished in the blast. The enemy might as well have ripped his heart from his chest.

Robert returned to his hometown weeks later with full access to all the army resources that he needed to help him adapt to the amputation. But despite everyone's best efforts, it became the most onerous experience of his life. How could he resume a life that no longer existed?

The experience didn't only alter his physical appearance; Robert changed dramatically on the inside as well. Though aware that it was contrary to his previous attitude, he was very angry. Why had this happened to him? Inevitably, he slipped into a depression from which he struggled to recover.

His parents offered as much support as they could. "Bobby," volunteered his mom, "why don't you go with your dad to the mall? Getting out might help you change your spirits some."

"I don't feel like it," he moaned.

"But you've got to get out a little. Staying cooped up in here is not good for you."

"Staying cooped up in here is what I should have done instead of getting my leg blown off!"

"It's not your fault," claimed his dad. "War is unjust, and people get hurt. How could they think we'll fix a problem over there by creating more problems over here?"

The question was rhetorical, of course. But the fact that his dad gave voice to it got Robert thinking. Maybe part of the solution was to focus on something other than the problem. If armed conflict was the cause of his amputation, what was the cause of the armed conflict? And what was the cause before that? What effect did we want to create anyway? And what other ways could we achieve that? Once he started asking these questions, he inevitably starting searching for the answers as well.

Robert knew that he also needed help to resolve his emotions. Many months later, with the benefit of intense counseling, he finally started to accept his condition. He came to the realization that he had to make new choices. What was he going to do with the rest of his life as an amputee?

He began looking at the options he had in the army and was presented with a variety of office jobs, each one more or less mundane in comparison to the questions he asked and the answers he sought. He recalled the support, encouragement, and solace that he'd received from the army chaplain during his darkest hours at the army's medical facility. He also remembered the counseling that he received from the army's chaplain back home. He then engaged in a new recognizance trip of an entirely different kind.

His decision became obvious and easy from that point forward. He enrolled in a chaplaincy program with financial assistance from the army, and today he provides the same kind of support, encouragement, and solace to other army reservists that he received in his time of need. The answers to his questions were reflected in a place he never anticipated—the eyes of the soldiers he counseled.

Robert summed up his transformation in his own words. "I don't worry about the forces of our enemies any longer. I focus on the strengths of our brave troops. I may have lost a leg to intelligence work, but I found my heart again as a chaplain."

Joel's Gift

I found a home away from home

Ana Barlow

As told to Ana by her friend Joel

THE BARLOWS KNEW we were in need of a break from our family when they invited my brothers and me to spend the rest of the summer with them. They were nearing the end of a cross-country trip through the United States. My home state of California was one of their last stops before heading back home to Texas. I was thrilled! It was the summer before my freshmen year in high school, and I had managed to waste my break playing video games and picking on my younger brother. Sure, I'll go on a trip even if it means riding in a car for thousands of miles. Besides, things were not going well at home, and the constant arguing between my parents was taking a toll on all of us. I had long given up on the jet skiing trip our Dad had promised. If I got lucky, he'd agree to drive my buddies and me to the lake without too much begging. I planned to have as little contact with my dad as possible for the rest of the summer.

My brothers and I threw a few things in a bag, and joined the Barlows. After just a few hours in the car we caught on to the spirit of adventure. I thought it was crazy to take a family of seven and two dogs in a car for eleven thousand miles, definitely something my family would never do. In our family, deciding what radio station to listen to alone would make us want to kill one another.

All of that was behind me for the next few weeks. I planned to get a lot of reading done and maybe have a fling with a southern belle. Little did I know that our next stop in Idaho would change my summer plans and start my life off in a whole new direction.

We stopped to visit with the Barlows' friends the Alexanders. They represented everything I've ever wanted in a family but could not have. Right away, the warmth of their country house made me glad to be there. Mr. and Mrs. Alexander gave me a genuine welcome, and I saw them interacting with each other in such a loving way.

My first evening there I was enjoying a conversation with one of their daughters when we heard her dad coming up from downstairs singing and playing his guitar. His eyes sparkled with kindness and humor. I could picture myself as a little kid sitting on his lap while he strummed his guitar.

"That's so cool. I wish I could play the guitar. I just don't have enough money to get one," I said.

"Here, why don't I show you a few chords?" He sat down on the couch next to me and played the D chord, and then he handed me the guitar. The weight of the guitar on my lap seemed to crush the excitement that arose within me. I wasn't exactly nervous, just slightly unsure of my ability. Trying to impress my dad was like trying to impress Michelangelo with finger painting. Nothing was ever good enough for him, so after a while I just stopped trying. I had to remind myself that there was no one I had to impress here. Mr. Alexander's relaxed presence eased my tension, and I was able to strum the D chord with confidence.

"Very good! You're a natural." He showed me a few more chords and watched patiently as I tried to repeat them. He didn't get frustrated when I messed up, and I felt comfortable with him even though we were practically strangers. I don't know how long we sat there working at the guitar together, but everyone was already in bed by the time we finished.

The next day, I spent some more one-on-one time with Mr. Alexander. I could be honest with him about anything, and he genuinely understood and wanted to listen to my dreams and thoughts. His responses were always filled with wisdom. Instead of belittling me as my father was prone to do, he made me feel like a man. I had grown used to filtering out the negative things that my dad had to say because I knew that most of it was not true. I feared that if I listened to him, I would eventually become like him. I wanted to listen to Mr. Alexander, and hoped that his words would mold my character and someday inform my parenting. I wished that Mr. Alexander and I had time for more than just a few chords on the guitar.

The road trip was coming to an end, and it was time to make the long haul back to Texas. There were thirteen of us sprawled out in sleeping bags downstairs on the morning we were planning to leave. We had spent our last night together watching movies and cracking jokes till the wee hours of the night. I rubbed my sleepy eyes and tried to wake up. My hands fell back on the floor and crunched the popcorn scattered all around me. Dreading the long trip in the car that lay ahead, I managed to crawl out of my sleeping bag. I stood up and noticed that there was a guitar case propped up against the piano right next to where I was sleeping. Taped to it was a folded note with my name on it. I looked around to see if anyone else was in on this and then opened the note.

> Joel,
> I saw that you have a great desire to play the guitar, and from the way you played those chords I showed you, I believe you will have much success at it before long. I think you have a talent that the Lord will use for his glory. Please take this guitar as a gift from the Lord and have lots of fun with it—I did.
> I think you're an upstanding young man, and I'm excited to hear about you and your accomplishments in the future. Please keep in touch.

I stood there shocked, unable to fully comprehend what I had just read. I felt so undeserving. A part of me could not accept such a gift. After all, I was just like any other teenage boy who dreamed of playing guitar and becoming a rock star. Except those boys usually saved every penny that they earned by mowing lawns and doing chores to buy their first guitar. I never even cared much for music. Yet I knew that this guitar was the start of something special, a dream I would pursue for the rest of my life.

It has been almost four years since I first strummed the chords of that guitar. I now own four guitars. I became the worship leader for the youth group at my church. Just recently, a prestigious college granted me a large scholarship to pursue a minor in music. To this day, Mr. Alexander has been my only instructor. He approached music with love and gentleness, something to be enjoyed, savored, and shared with others. Playing the guitar for others is one of the small ways I can pass on his generosity.

The Biggest Loser

If you can't do it for yourself,
do it for your family

Peter Victor

'M A BIG guy. I have always been big. I have never considered myself to be overweight—I'm simply a big dude. Other people think that I'm overweight. In fact, the two words that are most commonly used to describe me are *morbidly obese*. I am, and always have been, comfortable with who I am: Peter the big teacher from Bangor, Maine.

The biggest pain in the neck about being obese is doctors' reactions. It seemed as if they were always getting on me. I remember the jerk of a doctor I saw when I was sixteen years old. He told me that I would not see my twenty-first birthday. Heck, I was only 200 pounds. I remember thinking that if I have to die young, I'll die young. That's fine with me. It's the quality of a life that matters, not the quantity. I am fine.

Well, that doctor was wrong. My twenty-first birthday came and went, and it seems that I am still alive and feeling fine. But, I do have to admit that I have not always felt fine. I remember how I felt after being told that I had to purchase two tickets to attend University of Maine hockey games. I guess the two words that described my feelings best were hurt and humiliated. I could not afford two tickets!

Being turned away from hockey games does not compare to what I went through at the dentist. I stopped going to the dentist for more than six years. Why? Because I could not fit into the chair! The embarrassment was too much, so I left the office, avoiding the look on the dentist's face. I swore then that I would never go back.

First it was the hockey games and then the dentist, but what really shook me up was when I realized how my weight issue was affecting my family. Visits to the hospital were becoming a regular event. Most often these visits were due to cellulite, and the doctors could not cure me—I had too much weight!

I left the hospital that last time with a new prescription. My brother is a doctor, so I told him what I had been given. Then he asked my sister in Michigan what she thought. She's a research pharmacist. Shortly thereafter I learned that while my sister was in labor with her first child, she was on the phone with my brother frantically telling him that I had been prescribed the wrong medication. It was bad enough that I had missed her wedding, but now she was in labor with her first child and in a hysterical panic. A birth is supposed to be a very special time, and I was ruining it for her. I knew then things had to change.

I had never imagined that my weight would become an issue to my family. I now realized that it had and that I was a negative influence on their lives. This realization devastated me! I knew that my family loved me and that my weight-related issues and problems were tearing them apart. So one night, I sat in my bathroom with my head in my hands and tears in my eyes and understood that I had to change.

I visited my doctor to ask what could be done. He told me that one option was a gastric bypass. He said things were almost to the point where it was mandatory. He asked me to discuss it with my family and then meet with a dietician. I decided to visit the dietician first.

I had not expected the dietician to be as blunt and direct as she was. At first, her tone and choice of words did not seem helpful to me. But in hindsight, she was not the first professional to think that I was going to die soon. I guess she had never seen a 780-pound man before.

Twenty-two hundred calories a day! I was staggered as I listened to the dietician suggest this diet as a last-ditch attempt to avoid surgery. I usually consumed more than two thousand calories in one meal! But heck, I had to give it a try, although I wasn't going to tell anyone. I was already taking enough grief and did not want anyone looking at me and saying, "He couldn't stay the course."

I looked at the reading on the scale. In one week, I had lost fifteen pounds! I began to research and take charge of my diet. I knew that I had to begin exercising. And the weight continued to come off.

I knew that moment was only the beginning, and it was. Since that time, more than six years ago, I have lost another 485 pounds. The over-sized scale has been given away.

My weight issue had impacted my family more than I knew. I had always wondered why my younger sister in New York never spoke to me. She recently confessed that she did not want to get too close to me because she thought it would be too painful when I died. We now talk to each other every Sunday.

The first glance through my frosted window tells me everything I need to know—it is cold. Six degrees! Yes, this is cold by anyone's standard. I am going to need my over-sized mitts and my ski mask this morning. But it is March already. Soon I will be making these pre-dawn six-mile walks wearing shorts and a sweatshirt. These walks are important. Even though my weight has been stable for more than a year, there is much to do in the way of cardiovascular health and muscle toning. When you lose five hundred-pounds, it leaves some holes and wrinkles. Take it from me—I know. I walked briskly down the cold, deserted street and thought about the five hundred pounds I'd lost.

It all began with the realization that I was negatively affecting my family. This realization provided me with the strength and motivation to take charge of my life. My life and the life of my loved ones have greatly improved as a result; I will never look back—ever.

Scars from the Past

Love truly is thicker than blood

Lucy Parker Watkins

NOTHING MADE SENSE to me when I was a child; it just didn't add up. No matter how hard I tried, I was unable to understand either my life or my circumstances. As a result, I lived with the ever-present feeling of dejection in an emotional condition stuck somewhere between second-best and worst. In my heart I knew that my world was messed up, but I just couldn't seem to change it.

Events in my adult life continued to perpetuate that feeling of unworthiness. With little to go on, I continued to seek validation and answers. Sadly, I usually turned to the wrong people. All I ever wanted was to feel loved, to be acknowledged, and to feel worthy. Two marriages, three affairs, and two divorces later, I understood love to be fleeting and painful. I never thought I was good enough for anything better, but I always wanted more.

Despite years of therapy in the offices of many trusted counselors, I never confessed to my childhood habit of self-harm. Cutting had been my method of choice. It wasn't until Thanksgiving 2007 that the bloody memories of my youth and some newfound understanding flooded every cell of my being.

I was sitting on a neighbor's porch talking to a troubled thirteen-year-old girl who reminded me of my younger self. The connection I felt with this person was intense and in-explicable, for I barely knew her. I knew that she was smart, but I also knew that she, like me, sought unhealthy love from outside her home in an attempt to feel worthy.

As the girl rose from her chair, the bracelets covering her thin wrists moved higher up her arms. That's when I saw the scars—the telltale signs of self-loathing. Instantly, I flashed back to the blue-and-white bathroom of my grandmother's house, where I cut myself for the first time, and I immedi-ately understood the marks on the girl's arm and her quiet expression of pain.

I reached out and held the girl's wrist and then gently caressed the scars with my hand.

"What's this?" I asked softly. The girl allowed me to con-tinue holding her arm. She looked me in the eyes, glanced down at her scars, and then directly into my eyes again and said,

"Oh, those? I don't do it any more."

"Neither do I," I responded.

The girl was visibly stunned. Her eyes locked in a gaze with mine. She then looked down at my hand as I continued to caress her cutting marks. The girl lowered her gaze to her feet as though in shame. Not quite knowing what to say, I told her, "Just know that I'm here when you need me."

It was at that moment that I understood why I felt a con-nection with this young girl. We were more alike than was visible on the surface; we both wanted to feel loved and worthy. We didn't understand our lives, and we didn't know how to get what we wanted, but in that instant I was able to utter words that I'd always wanted to hear someone say to me.

Later, as I thought about my cutting days, I began to discern the course of my life and some of the solutions that I needed to correct it. By seeing myself in this girl and then discovering that we shared a dark and dangerous secret, I knew what I had to do for myself. I needed to love the little girl that I was in the way I wanted others to love me. I had to help her feel good enough. So I quietly said to my younger self, "You are worthy. You are special. You are loved."

My skin prickled as I uttered those words I had craved forever. As my eyes filled with tears, I sat on the couch, closed my eyes, wrapped my arms around myself, and bawled. In my mind's eye, I saw the little girl that I was, sitting in her grandmother's bathroom, cutting and tearing at her small hands, mourning the loss of her mother to cancer, and depleted by the pain of her father's theft of her innocence through his perverted notions of what a daughter is supposed to do for a father.

I recalled the intensity of the pain and the weight of the insecurity, but then something flickered in my mind. I saw the faces of my past teachers, my childhood friends, my grandmother and grandfather, my aunt, my sisters, and many others who had reached out to me when I was a child. I tried to understand why I didn't allow them to affect me all those years ago. Slowly I realized that I had been frightened by the potential for more loss and suffering. I was terrified of loving and losing yet again. Even at the age of ten, I was convinced that love was fleeting, love was painful, and love was a pipedream.

Exhausted from the emotional upheaval I felt from this revelation, I realized that there was more to do. Even though saying those words to my younger self was cathartic, it wasn't enough. I suddenly realized that my lifelong focus had always been to find love outside myself. Of course that type of love had the potential of being fleeting, especially since I didn't consider myself worthy of the words "I love you." The sincerity behind that phrase had been inconsequential to me.

The measure of my worth had always come from the way I was treated by the people who hurt me the most, not from those strong, loving, healthy people who actually made appearances in my life. And the one person I'd never asked to love me was myself.

As I sat alone with my thoughts, loving the little girl that I was, I finally began to feel love and compassion for the woman I had become. There was only one thing to do. I made my way to the bathroom, gazed at my reflection, and looked deeply into the eyes of the woman I saw before me. She had survived sexual abuse, the deaths of loved ones, her father's raging alcoholism, two divorces, and many other unnamed events. To the reflection I said, "You are worthy. You are special. You are loved."

Because I saw the heart of a young girl who bore slash marks on her arms, this one moment of clarity rang through the craziness of my own life. This instant led me to the one earthly being who could love me unconditionally, with an understanding of my intentions and my choices. That person was me. Who would have thought that a girl, saying little more than "I don't do it any more" could have brought forth such a life-changing moment? I surely didn't. As a result, I am now my own woman.

I face the struggles and challenges of single parenting with a sense of determination, rather than victimization. I move forward and grow with each new experience. Before seeing that girl's arms, every new challenge felt insurmountable. And although I have my moments of insecurity, regret, loneliness, and fear, I am forever changed. I am focused on learning to love myself as I've always prayed others would love me. Ultimately this act also has helped my children feel the love they deserve.

When I look back on my life, I can list the exact circumstances and number of times when my father said he loved me. He said it four times during my life. But, as I sit here now, I can't accurately count the number of friends who love me as one of their own. I also can't count the number of hugs I receive every day. And I can't count the number of times I hear "thank you" and "I love you." Seeing that girl's arms took me on a journey I never dreamed I would take. Now I can honestly and sincerely say, *"I am worthy. I am special. I am loved."*

You've Got Mail

When the virtual world gets real

Julie Adler Rosen

IT WAS FEBRUARY of 1995, before the birth of the worldwide web as we now know it. If you weren't a computer geek at a university, then your only Internet options were AOL, Prodigy, and CompuServe. The Internet service providers were just getting off the ground, and AOL pursued potential customers by bombarding them with free trial discs in the mail.

I was in graduate school, and in between classes I went to see my advisor. She asked me to wait while she finished an email to a friend in Israel. I had no idea what she was talking about; we were in Los Angeles and she was sitting at her computer, so how was she doing anything with someone in Israel? She explained the concept, and I found it absolutely intriguing. My best friend from college traveled for work, and I figured now we'd be able to stay in touch while she was hopping around the globe.

Later that night, I loaded an AOL disc into my computer and logged on for the first time. I had no idea what I was doing and no idea how to put my new AOL account to use. My first thought was to search for some information.

But what did I want to know? Something really pressing. Something I couldn't wait to find out. Aha! When were the

Grateful Dead going to play in Las Vegas? This was information of the highest priority indeed. Actually, it was February, and the Vegas shows weren't until the summer, but I was dying to know anyway.

Deadheads always know where the Dead are and where they will be in the near future. I began to appreciate the value of AOL and the Internet. I managed to find a Grateful Dead Forum and asked these virtual Deadheads about the Vegas show dates. I got several responses, one of which came from IROSEN. I decided to send IROSEN a "message" to see what would happen. I said "hi" and IROSEN replied "hi."

Hmmmm. That was weird, but cool.

So then I "emailed" IROSEN to see how it worked.

IROSEN wrote back.

We started a "pen pal" correspondence and shared information about our daily lives. After a few exchanges, IROSEN tried to set me up with his friend's sister at my grad school.

He assumed I was a guy. It was so funny, because I was sure that I was coming across as a girl in our emails. Didn't my writing voice sound female?

Well, I wrote him back and thanked him for his offer, but I explained that I liked my dates "tall, dark, handsome, and preferably male." He didn't respond, and I thought perhaps I'd messed up my email. I was still new to AOL and the Internet, so I resent the message.

He replied and said that he was so embarrassed about mistaking me for a guy that he just wasn't going to email random people on AOL any more.

It's a good thing I persisted with my emails, because had I not, I never would have found the love of my life. IROSEN and I have been married for eleven years, and we have two amazing sons. I always say our virtual paths crossed in a virtual world. My dad says it was *bashert* (meant to be).

Threads of Ink

A writer finds her voice

Dylene Cymraes

I STARED OUT THE window at stubborn gray raindrops falling like persistent tears from a heavy sky. My own tears welled up in my eyes,and my throat felt hot and choked, as if I'd swallowed a fist. An emotional storm raged in my eight-year-old mind. My Grandma Eve sat on stiff cushions that would later form a bed in the small travel trailer, which slept five, if they didn't mind listening to one another breathe. My Grandpa Pete called the trailer the *Little Nomad*, with a play on the words. "No one can be angry in the *No*-Mad," he'd say with a silly look on his face. But Grandpa Pete wasn't there that day. Grandma looked at me with thinly veiled impatience and bookmarked her textbook. She was burying herself in study to continue her work as a special education teacher. My little sister, Wendy, thumped the bench with her heals in a monotonous rhythm. Like a petulant blonde angel, her usually bright blue eyes were dull and distant. The three of us were locked together in this small space. No doubt Grandma had taken us to the lake to try to get some peace of mind.

Despite Grandma Eve's effort, there was little peace of mind to be found. My mother, Grandma Eve's daughter, Vonnie, had died the previous year at the age of twenty-sex.

After she died, it seemed as though the surviving family members could see one another but not touch—the bridge between them had been swept away. Grief erected iron bars between us. Grandma turned to drink and frantic activity. Grandpa stayed alone in the garage and immersed himself in work. I retreated to the woods near our house in search of a world that still made sense. Wendy was left alone with the fantasy that Mommy would still come through the door any minute. The time since Mom's death sometimes seemed like years, other times like minutes, depending on how raw the wound felt.

Several months after Mom's death, Grandma took us to the lake. The television in our trailer broadcast only static, and the red-clay soil outside was a sticky soup. The three of us were trapped inside a tiny jail cell masquerading as a vacation trailer. "Play some cards," Grandma Eve had suggested earlier, "and drink your hot chocolate."

"I burned my tongue, and the marshmallows are all gone," Wendy said.

"I'm sick of cards," I retorted. "Wendy cheats."

"I do not!" Wendy gave me a vicious kick under the table. I reached out and yanked off her shoe, twisting her foot. She burst into tears, and suddenly Grandma Eve leapt up. She snapped her book shut.

In the small space, it sounded like a gunshot. "That's *enough*!" In exasperation, Grandma yanked a drawer open and pulled out a couple of yellow legal pads. She tossed a handful of pencils and dried-out markers on the laminate table. "Just draw, or write something." That was the last straw. Criticized

for my horrible cursive at school, the last thing I wanted to do
was *write* something. Tears spilled over my freckled cheeks. I
glared at Grandma, and the pent-up emotions erupted.

*"I don't know what they teach you to make kids do in that
school, but I don't have to do it!"* I declared, with all the vehemence I could muster.

I crossed my skinny arms over my chest. Looking back now,
it felt as if I was trying to keep the edges of my heart close
enough to hang on a little longer. Wendy looked dismally at
the legal pad before reaching out and taking a pencil. She
dutifully copied letters from a box of crackers. Her words
staggered along the page in the crooked, spidery font of a
young child.

I was angry about being shoved aside—again—when I just
wanted to tell someone how much I hurt. My legs were stick-
ing to the vinyl seat; I was hot and cold, and miserable inside
my own skin. The one person who could hug me and make
it all better was gone forever. I slumped into the corner and
looked outside. Grandma Eve picked up her book again.

"Suit yourself," she said, "but let me finish this chapter."
I sat and sulked for as long as my tomboy self could stand
the inactivity. I snatched up a felt-tipped pen and looked at
the lake, far down the path, covered with dancing gray fog. I
watched birds huddled against wet bark, so close that if the
window had been open, I could have touched their feathers.
A cut branch bled sap in milky amber drops. I thought about
how clean and fresh it must smell outside—blue Colorado sky
washed by afternoon rain. Scaly pine bark would feel soft on
my fingers when I climbed the trees later. Golden powdery

pollen would gather on puddles. The ache in my throat eased and the tears dried.

To my surprise, I looked down and saw that I had been *writing*. I had written about two deer I saw in my mind, by a moonlit pond on a still, quiet night. Complete fiction. I don't know what words I used. All I remember is my Grandma's look of genuine surprise when she read the work, and her words. "This is really *good*. You should write some more." My *thin thread* moment came in the hurried slap of a legal pad and some barely serviceable pens and pencils on a table. It came as something, *anything*, to occupy a bored, frustrated, and emotionally wounded child long enough for her grandma to finish what she felt was the most important thing at the time— studying for a college exam in a program she never finished. It came from a woman haunted by grief for her only daughter, a woman overwhelmed by the sudden responsibility for two little girls while she was in mid-menopause and thought the reward of retirement was just around the corner.

Most of all, it came when my first literary critic took the time to make out my messy penmanship and get to the underlying meaning. Instead of telling me my letters were sloppy, she told me that what I had done was worthy of praise.

I started writing at the age of eight. I am now forty-six. I have since written screenplays, novels, a biography, countless articles, and press releases. I continue to be mesmerized by the magic of words, the dance of letters that communicate, challenge, and inspire. I have stolen time to fill notebooks while my children were fast asleep, and written story ideas on napkins and receipts. I have found myself moved to tears by a well-crafted line of prose. There have been times when the little flame of faith has nearly been snuffed out by writer's fears, but somehow this part of my soul has survived. I am a writer.

I found my calling in that *thin thread* moment when Grandma Eve chose to challenge me on a rainy day with a blank sheet of legal paper.

Dreams Can Come True

A family's turning point
and triumph over autism

Susan Lynn Perry

I'D LIKE TO paint a picture for you. Let me set the scene. Try to imagine, if you will, that you are the mother of a beautiful little baby boy. This baby is such a blessing to you because you didn't believe that you were able to get pregnant. You and your husband had tried and tried in the past, but to no avail.

Then, lo and behold, when you least expect it, you are indeed pregnant. Your pregnancy is wonderful, and you are lucky enough to be robust and healthy throughout the entire nine months. Your baby is born perfectly healthy with ten little fingers and ten little toes. Everyone in your family is overjoyed at your perfect little bundle.

Now, imagine that your baby gets sick. In fact, he's suddenly sick all of the time, with ear infections, bronchitis, upper respiratory infections, vomiting, diarrhea, allergies, eczema, unexplained fevers, and colds. Every week, it's another sickness. His doctor isn't concerned, so you try not to be either.

Then, imagine that his vocabulary and language, which had increased to several words, stops progressing all together. Imagine that your perfect little boy stops putting his hands out when he falls at home and on the playground. He seems dizzy, distracted, and disoriented most of the time. Imagine that he stops responding to his name or responding to you, his mother, at all.

His doctor says he's just fine, but you know better. You start asking around and reading and researching. You have your suspicions but hope to God they are not true. Then finally, several months or even years later, you are given the devastating diagnosis of autism. And not only that, but you are then faced with some even more horrifying news:

There is no cure for autism.

No cure? How can an otherwise normal child be suddenly thrust into a world from which there's no hope of return? This is what I was faced with during the first four years of my son's life. Countless other families are getting that same diagnosis every minute of every day with this growing worldwide epidemic. Statistics are now showing that one in ninety-four boys is being diagnosed with autism. Sounds pretty grim, doesn't it?

When I was given this news over a year ago, I was understandably heartbroken and upset. But, then I got to work. I refused to believe that there was nothing I could do to help bring my son back to my world. I dreamed of a time when I would hear my little boy tell me he loved me without it simply being an automated repetition of my words.

I wanted to hear him say it—of his own volition and free will. I wanted him to feel it and to believe it. I wanted to see that look in his eyes and to know in my mother's heart that he meant it.

Parents who have never dealt with this disorder have no idea what it's like to have your son look right past you when you walk into a room to stare at something or someone else moving around in the background. Your child is *your* world, and for most young children, their parents are *their* world. When it comes to children with autism, however, their worlds are all jumbled and chaotic. They often have trouble focusing on anyone, including their parents.

For a mother, that cuts right to the core of your very being.

I made the decision over a year ago that no matter what the cost, emotionally, physically and/or financially, I would try and keep trying until I brought my Justin back. This is probably the hardest thing I've ever done, but I know I will keep going as long as I must, now that I've seen the light at the end of the tunnel. It grows brighter every day, and I know that one day very soon we will step out of the tunnel completely.

I began this journey by researching as much information about the condition as I could find on the Internet. I immediately understood that when a child's system has been damaged by illness, genetics, or an environmental cause such as heavy-metal toxicity, the easiest place to start seeing improvements is by enhancing his or her immune system. So that's where I began.

I learned about nutritional supplements that would bolster the immune system and began supplementing Justin's diet with some of them.

I began to see improvements in behavior and eye contact almost immediately.

Next, I knew we needed to find a specialist who could really pinpoint what was going on in Justin's body. I did research to find a DAN! doctor, which stands for Defeat Autism Now!, and found one about an hour from our house. I made my first appointment and filled out all of the patient intake information prior to that appointment.

I pulled together all of Justin's past doctor, pharmacy, and specialist receipts and put together a medical timeline of every sickness he had experienced and the resulting treatment received. This timeline began to give me a very clear picture of just how sick my little boy had been. It also helped the new doctor have a crystal-clear understanding of Justin's medical past and the treatments that might help him start to recover.

We added more nutritional supplements, speech therapy, B12 shots, a gluten-free, caffeine-free diet, and several medical tests to his regimen. With each step, we began to unravel the mystery of our son's autism. The bottom line was that he'd had an adverse reaction to his vaccinations that overloaded his immune system. Since his immune system was compromised, he could not fight off common childhood illnesses. The doctors had him on an enormous amount of antibiotics in early childhood, causing mammoth gastrointestinal distress. All of these things slowed down his development, which resulted in his eventual diagnosis of autism.

As we were able to piece together the complicated puzzle of his deteriorating health, we were able to treat each issue one by one. As each issue was treated, we received substantial and measurable results in the form of improved health, better nutrition, increased awareness, eye contact, better behavior, and overall growth.

Next, we started a therapy called chelation, which is a process to remove heavy metals from the body. We continued to see spectacular results. Finally, we added a therapy called Hyperbaric Oxygen Therapy, which forces oxygen into some of the damaged areas of his brain and body. We anticipate this being the final piece of therapy for this very intricate puzzle of autism recovery.

When we were given the diagnosis over a year ago, we were told, "Your son has autism. There is no cure." What we were not told, however, is that it *is* possible to recover from autism, one step at a time. It is a long, tiring, expensive journey. There have been many days when I feel like throwing in the towel and never looking back, but then something miraculous always happens to give me the strength I need to keep going. Like three months ago, when Justin looked into my eyes one night as I finished reading him a bedtime story, touched my cheek softly, and said, "Mommy, I love you *so* much."

And you know what? I knew in my heart of hearts that he meant it.

An Angel with Four Legs

The power of people and prayer

Mary I. Russo

LOOKING THROUGH SOME family files, I recently came across a 1958 newspaper clipping. It brought back memories of an experience that proved to me God is watching, protecting, and sending his angels to care for us. A security guard and three teenage boys, who would be in their sixties now, would likely have more to add to the story. They were in the right place at the right time, helping a neighborhood look for a missing child.

Usually my five-year-old brother Ricky would be inside while Mom was preparing dinner, but the late afternoon sun was too tempting after a long rainy day. Mom could watch my two younger brothers from the kitchen window overlooking the backyard. I was doing my homework in my bedroom.

I could hear the boys playing with our shepherd collie, Prince. We all loved that dog, but he seemed to pay particularly close attention to Ricky. Could a dog know that Ricky had Down's Syndrome?

Our street was a valley, which made the back of our yard a hill of rising shrubs and trees that stretched to the street beyond. Dad walked home from work, and often arrived home at 3:45 P.M., emerging from the trees as if birthed by

112

the forest. It was getting close to his arrival time, and Mom called me to the table.

There was an odd silence in the kitchen when I got there, quickly followed by Mom's nervous voice calling Ricky and Prince from the back porch. Then came a whistle that skipped across her lips until she ran out of breath. Where was Ricky? My youngest brother, who was four at the time, could only tell us that Prince went with Ricky.

I'll never forget the fear in Mom's eyes as she ran through the neighborhood, calling for Ricky and Prince, enlisting any help that the questioning neighbors would offer. It quickly became a large search party, and Dad heard the commotion as he came down from the hill.

Mom cried on Dad's shoulder as she told him Ricky was missing. Dad wasted no time and called the police. In fear, Mom prayed aloud, *"Please God, don't let him wander toward the Wilbur Cross Parkway."*

When my grandparents arrived, my parents took the car and drove up and down the side streets. I knew God was with my brother.

Even though he couldn't talk very well, he could sure make a person feel loved. He hugged everybody. I knelt down beside my bed and prayed that someone would find Ricky before dark.

The telephone rang, and my grandmother raced to answer it. The police just wanted to know whether Ricky was wearing a red baseball cap, which he wasn't. She was told that a red cap had been found in a storm drain a few blocks from our house.

As I watched my grandmother's shoulders sag, tears began to stream down her face. I knew she was losing hope, and I had to do something. I convinced my grandmother to let me go with some friends to look for Ricky at the park, only four blocks away. He loved the "shooty-shoot," and he would sit on the seesaw just waiting for someone to come along and "make it go," but no one at the park had seen him.

Most of the police officers who went off duty at 6:00 P.M. kept looking for my brother. One of these kind men spotted a mother comforting her crying child on Grandview Avenue, the street over the hill.

The mother explained that a boy had come along and sat on her child's bike. She said that the boy rode down the hill toward Dixwell Avenue. There was a dog with him, and the boy called him Prince.

WELI, a local Hamden-based radio station, picked up on the story. Reports began coming in of a boy fitting Ricky's description seen crossing the busy main street of Dixwell Avenue. Earlier on that same street, a guard at the High Standard Manufacturing Corporation noticed a young boy and a dog walking around, but he didn't think anything of it until he heard the radio broadcast.

The sun was beginning to set when the guard looked out back and saw a dog circling a cinder pit in the work yard of the Plasticrete Corporation next door. Unable to leave his post the guard summoned three teenage boys who were walking by the work yard. He asked them to see why the dog's bark was so frantic.

"Me want out!" Ricky's panic-stricken voice echoed as he clawed at the walls of the twenty-foot pit.

Prince was still barking and pacing along the edge of the hole when the boys found Ricky in the pit. The boys knew that if they didn't act quickly, Ricky would continue to pull cinders over himself and could suffocate.

After reassuring Prince that they wouldn't harm Ricky, the boys stretched out to make a human chain down the side of the pit and lifted Ricky to safety.

The crowd stepped aside as the flashing blue lights approached the curb in front of our house. Mom tore right through the screen door as she burst outside to hug Ricky.

Tears of joy washed over Ricky's face, all covered with charcoal, as he was smothered with affection. The policeman said it was a good thing Prince refused to abandon Ricky, because the delivery trucks just back up to the pits and dump the coal. Without knowing, they would have buried him alive! We were all hugging Prince when Ricky said, *"Puppy, ice cream?"*

"Ice cream and anything else he wants!" Mom answered with a laugh.

On the local TV program *Happy the Clown*, Prince was awarded a medal for his faithfulness. Prince has since passed away, but I believe this angel still stands guard beside Ricky fifty years later.

A Wish List for Mr. Right

How I found
the perfect man for me

Kathy Shiels Tully

W HEN WE WERE in our early thirties, my girlfriends and I regularly complained about being single. It seemed that there were "no good men" out there. Why were *we* single? We enjoyed good careers, were college educated, and attractive.

Bethany had bouncy blonde hair, played the flute like a pro, and skied like an angel. Marybeth, a brunette banker, was serious on the outside and hid her hysterically funny self behind pinstripes.

Laila, a pretty preppy with a big, toothy smile, nursed her crushed heart from a recent broken engagement. I was financially independent, popular, and owner of a condo.

"You scare the men away, Kathy," Violet, an older woman in our department, warned me.

Then she added, "They must wonder, 'what can she want from me?'" Well, they couldn't have been more wrong.

At the age of thirty-one, for the first time, I wanted someone really special in my life. I was tired of the dating scene and tired of our weekly "sit and bitch" sessions. How many weekend nights had we wasted drinking chilled Chardonnay and complaining? It was time to change our M.O. As another round of rants began one Friday night, I interrupted Marybeth and challenged her.

"What are you looking for in a man?" Quickly, she rattled off five or six qualities as though she was reciting the Girl Scout pledge.

"Handsome, kind, good job, money, good to his mother, funny."

Next was Laila. Stuck in the muck of memories of her former fiancé, she couldn't focus on her future.

Bethany listed the same qualities that Marybeth had, adding one or two of her own. I wanted the same. How redundant?

Perhaps this was part of our problem. We were checking off generic qualities that you'd find on a dating-club questionnaire instead of pinpointing those qualities specific to our individual needs.

Obviously, we were all different from one another. I knew that if we met the same man possessing all of those qualities, only one of us would be interested, and maybe none of us would be. An idea formed in my head. Grabbing a yellow legal pad and a pen, I imagined myself as Mike Wallace from *60 Minutes* and announced that I was going to sharply interview each of my friends.

"I think we need to focus more on what we really, *really* want in a man. What's actually a priority and non-negotiable for you? You can list only ten qualities for your Mr. Right. Spell out what each adjective means to you. For example, if you list handsome, then explain what handsome means to you. I'll write it down."

Bethany volunteered to go first. Having a friend was important to her.

"What do you mean by 'friend'?" I asked. Pausing, she defined a friend as someone who was honest and someone to have fun with.

Catching on, she continued, "I want someone who's outdoorsy, athletic, and handsome. Most important, I want someone with kind eyes."

She was eager to have kids, and her mother shared this eagerness, so she was looking for someone who wanted a family.

"I want a man with a good job, but not necessarily in a corporation." Possessing her own entrepreneurial spirit, Bethany was open to her man having one too. Before long, she hit ten qualities and wanted to keep going.

"No, just the ten most important to you," I said.

"Decide whether there's anything you want to add or subtract." I ripped off the piece of paper with her top ten and gave it to her.

Laila's thoughts were scattered, so I gave her a welcomed reprieve. Marybeth was ready, but, once again, she rattled off a generic list of characteristics. She played along, but she was playing it safe. When I pushed her to more clearly define her descriptions, she demurred. Fine—if she wanted to be superficial, then that's what she'd get. I handed her the list.

Bethany took the legal pad and pen to interview me. I used the other lists as a guide, but I personalized them.

"I want someone who is a friend to me and to everyone. I want someone whom I find handsome, someone I could look at morning, noon, and night. But I don't want a man so handsome that other women will be looking at him and going after him." My friends laughed, knowing that I was a flirt.

"Religion is important to me too. Make that religious/ spiritual. I couldn't be with someone who doesn't believe in something greater than us. I want a man who is funny, who can make me laugh, but not a stand-up comedian. I also want someone who is outdoorsy and athletic, and who loves going to the beach and skiing." When I reached ten, Bethany shouted, "Done!"

"No. Since it was my idea, I get eleven." After they jokingly protested, I told them my bonus quality—someone who doesn't snore. No one else had even considered listing what she didn't want.

"We're talking marriage, the rest of our lives," I said. "I couldn't take a snorer." With my list done, Bethany ripped it off and handed it to me. Looking at my list, another idea hit me.

"Wait. One more thing—look at your lists. How many of these qualities do *you* possess? Be honest." Having a good job, but not necessarily a big money maker, was one of the qualities on my list.

I revised that quality to "has a job that he likes and does well." I believed that people who enjoy their professions are happier. Looking at my list, I realized that if I wanted that quality in him, then I needed to first find it in myself. Rolling up the scrap of paper, I stuffed it in my wallet.

Every so often, I would reread my list and think," Would I change anything? Have I developed the qualities on this list?"

Three months later, Bethany met Randy on a blind date set up by a co-worker. A hardcore skier and mountaineer, he dreamed of owning his own technology business. Although he was bald, you didn't notice because of his warm, brown eyes. They fell in love on their first date and married two years later.

Marybeth met Don, a wonderful man. He wanted to marry her. She refused. "He hunts. I couldn't marry someone who kills animals." Despite his other fine qualities, it was non-negotiable. They broke up.

Laila never focused. She kept changing jobs and men. She couldn't seem to forget her fiancé, even though he had long since left her.

My *Mr. Right* arrived in my life one year later. Still single at forty-three, he seemed created just for me. He was a man who had kept his friends since summer camp, who cared for his family. His sharp sense of humor showed that he listened and was smart. Unlike the slick guys I had previously dated, Joe was comfortable in his own skin and truly enjoyed his job. When talking to you, he focused on you, not others around you.

On our first date, we kissed for two hours. Was it nerves or just a long-awaited connection? After dating for two years, I found out that he was a snorer of the worst kind. Would this be a deal breaker? Nope. I simply crossed that quality off my list. There! Now he was perfect, for me. We married, and twelve years and two daughters later, he snores only occasionally.

The Stranger Who Saved a Life

We are strangers no more

Delores Liesner

RICHARD WAS NOTICEABLE even without his usual bright smile. Relatively new to this large, urban high school, I knew little of Richard except that he was active and well liked by everyone, including my boss, the Directing Principal.

I had learned that Richard had suffered a sudden heart attack and might have to limit activities for the rest of the year. Everyone knew that it would be especially difficult for Richard if he could not participate as usual in commencement.

I turned curiously from stuffing the mailboxes as I heard my boss greet Richard. I became alarmed at Richard's unusual lack of spirit when he explained that his doctor had ordered immediate retirement. Although barely acquainted, I felt compelled to connect with him, and I called out, "Richard, I'll be praying for you."

Turning in the doorway, he met my gaze. "Thanks," he said slowly, "but I feel like my life is over if I can't be with the students."

I was shocked that he would share such desperate thoughts with someone he barely knew. His words "my life is over" rang in my ears for weeks after. Uncomfortable about phoning a stranger, I begged the school psychologist and my boss to call Richard, but both sympathetically returned the burden. I finally accepted my boss's offer to "guard" my closed office door from interruption as I dialed Richard's number.

A last-minute attempt to talk with his wife failed when Richard himself answered the phone. He responded with a melancholy tone that his wife and girls were out picking up a few things for their trip to see family for Thanksgiving. Dumbly, I said, "Okay, I will call back later." My heart clenched in fear as I absorbed his emphasis that *they* were going rather than *we* were going. I was nodding my head in obedience when Richard's dull voice released a wall of emotion and buried memories of my Dad's depression after a heart attack.

"Richard," I confessed, "I asked to speak to your wife because I didn't know if you would speak with someone you barely know. But your reaction to your surgery reminded me of my dad, and I would like to tell you about him if you would listen." I shared how my dad loved his job and made it his life until a sudden heart attack weakened my "superhero." I recalled my father telling me how he felt as though he'd never be whole again. Richard was surprised to hear that he felt that way too. I continued to relate memories of how the family felt helpless as the strange enemy of depression locked my dad away from our reach.

My voice broke as I recalled our desperation to reach Dad. I wondered aloud whether Richard's wife and daughters felt as we did (like failures) because they couldn't seem to get through to him, just as we couldn't get through to our dad. Richard's voice slowly came to life. "Why I never imagined they might feel that way," he said thoughtfully.

I told Richard how my dad was touched when our seven-year-old wrote "John 3:16" on a card and carefully printed that he could "trust God to love him even more than any of our family could because he gave his Son to do what even Grandpa could not do for himself." Once Dad found hope in God's message, he was ready to listen to the doctor. I told Richard that the doctor's response was that depression was a normal side effect for many people after heart surgery and that it was nothing to be ashamed of. This fact encouraged me to ask Richard to make several promises.

I wanted him to join the family for Thanksgiving; to write down all that he felt God had done for him and had given him; and to call the doctor and check in with me when he got back. Richard said that he could put off his plans for that evening and he would report in after Thanksgiving. His promises gave me reassurance. The call ended, and my office door opened.

A speculative "How'd it go?" from my boss turned to astonishment when I said that I'd requested promises from Richard. Eventually, my boss felt assured that Richard would keep his word.

The following Tuesday morning, the phone rang and a jubilant Richard announced, "You were right; the doctor said that I have a side effect from surgery, and I am starting a prescription today." But this wasn't the only thanks I received. The first was in the form of a card from his daughter that said,

"We don't know all of what you shared with my dad, but that conversation changed his life. We have our daddy back." To think that I almost missed out on that blessing by being worried what someone would think of a stranger calling!

The second came the next morning, when my boss reacted in surprise as a familiar shadow filled the doorway with a smiling Richard. Richard had come on a mission and quickly revealed it as he pointed at me while querying the principal. "Did you know about her phone call?" he asked. As the principal nodded, Richard's direct glance held us breathless as he continued.

"Well, what she didn't know was that I had a gun ready that night, and I had plans to use it. It took a stranger to call me and wake me up."

The three of us were locked in a moment of startled silence, and then the words closest to my heart came to me. "But we are strangers no more," I said.

Shelly's Story

From adversity to achievement

Patrice Curtis

IN THE EARLY 1990s, I worked in the human resources department at a major university in Arizona. I knew first-hand that minority students who came from disadvantaged backgrounds faced a number of problems that could make it particularly difficult for them to complete their studies. Many of them didn't have good study habits; many didn't know how to dress for internship interviews; many had difficulty balancing independence and the challenges of a full course load.

Even though I was nearing the end of my career, I decided that I wanted to help them as best I could—so I transferred from my usual HR role to oversee a tutoring program for minority engineering students.

Shelly was one of a handful of young minority women in the program. She was a sophomore studying electrical engineering. Shelly stood out as one of the brightest students because of her smarts and attitude as well as her hard work. She had outstanding potential and a great personality; she was a true joy to be around.

Shelly was also a single mom with a four-year-old son, and, luckily, her parents helped by watching him when she was at class and doing her homework. They also contributed to Shelly's tuition and supported her and her son by letting them live at home. She was fortunate that she hadn't come from a background as disadvantaged as that of some of her peers.

One day toward the end of her sophomore year, Shelly came to see me in my office. She was close to tears and confessed that her parents told her they would not watch her son any more. In fact, they wanted her and her son to move out of their home and would no longer help with books and other tuition support.

Shelly was understandably distraught. Her parents' decision would be life-altering for her, and she admitted that she had to figure out how she was going to manage. She never told me why her parents had this radical change of mind, but it seemed that her mother was the driving force behind the decision. Perhaps a contributing factor was that her young son required more attention and guidance than they were able to give.

Although Shelly had won a partial scholarship, she said that she would have to drop out of school to get a job. She had been looking at available employment and had twisted herself inside out to find a solution that would allow her to continue her full-time studies. But there was just no way for her to continue. She declared that she would drop out of school as soon as she found a job, and maybe once everything sorted itself out, she would be able to enroll in night classes.

I was concerned for her, because I anticipated no way for her to manage working during the day and taking classes at night. Where would she find the hours needed to complete her homework? How would she balance all of that with caring for her son? If she had a different major and the studies were not as rigorous, maybe she could manage to get through somehow. But she was in engineering!

I was beside myself. I didn't like to lose any of my students, and Shelly was one of the best. I wouldn't let her quit if there was anything I could do about it.

Shelly exemplified the prime reason the tutoring program existed. She was a young woman with all the brainpower necessary to earn an engineering degree. We already had so few women in the program, and her grades were outstanding. Plus, she had a winning personality. There was no doubt in my mind that she would some day contribute to the world in a significant way.

An obvious solution to her dilemma would have been hiring her as a tutor for the same program in which she was enrolled. All the tutors at that time were upperclassmen—however, they were not themselves participants in the minority program. Shelly clearly did not fit that mold.

I looked into the resources I could readily offer her, and the hire option was all I could find. So I thought, "Why not?" Here was a student with excellent grades, who clearly understood the material and could easily appreciate the particular challenges that minority freshmen were facing. I decided to approach my manager about the idea.

Not surprisingly, my manager quizzed me endlessly about altering the way things had always been done. But the bottom

line was this: Did I think Shelly would be able to do the job?
She would have the potential success of many students in her
hands. Could she be an effective tutor?

Effective tutoring was critical to the academic success of
students in the program. Hiring Shelly could have many
repercussions. Thus I knew what my manager wanted from
me—I had to vouch for Shelly. Was I willing to stake my
reputation on the success of this idea?

My word was on the line, and I gave it readily, without
hesitation. I had complete confidence in Shelly's ability to
succeed. I was determined to see to it that the challenging
situation she was experiencing would not force her to leave
school.

To my great delight, she got the tutoring job. Her grandmother serendipitously stepped in to care for her son. Everything was in place to help her complete her studies.

What happened as a result? Shelly's first year of tutoring was a great success! The freshmen students she tutored
thought highly of her, and she became an inspiration and role
model for other young women at the university who were in
the heavily male-dominated world of electrical engineering.
In other words, Shelly successfully broke the mold for all the
tutors who came after her, showing that minority students
could tutor other minority students.

I retired from the university the summer before Shelly
became a senior, and thus I did not see her graduate. When
I left, she had completed her junior year with strong grades
and was going to be a tutor in her senior year as well. Best of
all, she was just nine months away from graduating.

I have all the confidence in the world that Shelly went on to get the job of her choice in engineering and provide her son with a strong role model. I also have no doubt that she is making the world a better place in her unique way. She may have been a minority student with a disadvantaged background, but she transformed all of that into a personal and professional advantage. The greatest difference she made, I believe, is that she left the university a better place. From what I hear, they still talk about Shelly's story.

Lightness

How my friend faced mortality

Jennifer Bunin

THE FRONT PORCH of David's house at school faces the east side of Home Avenue. The couch on the front porch is weather worn. David likes to sit and smoke, placing finished butts in an aged coffee can. The can has never been emptied, and to avoid addressing it, David tosses some of his finished cigarettes on the front lawn. From his seat he can see the bodies of people walking by his house, but not their faces. As both unfamiliar and familiar bodies pass, some with recognizable gaits, the wooden railing censors personalities and allows David to remain comfortably seated. Before I quit smoking, David would invite me to join him. On a particularly warm day last March, I came by uninvited, hoping to find David sitting in his usual spot and in want of some company. I was in luck. I lit a cigarette as I climbed the front steps and then sat down next to him and exhaled. I turned to him for a greeting, but his frontward gaze remained unbroken. The lit cigarette in his right hand had grown an ash nearly an inch long. Not a part of him moved. The ash finally caved in to gravity.

"David?"

"How much time do you have, Jen?"

"Enough."

"I heard somewhere that each one of these things takes about three minutes off your life."

"It's a good thing I'm nineteen and invincible." David flicked his cigarette into the yard. The ember burned for a few seconds before dying. "That guy I had a fling with over winter break called today. He just found out that he is HIV positive. We didn't use protection." My initial attempts at comforting him were in vain. I asked him only what I needed to know. David explained to me that he was going home to get tested that week, but even if the test came back negative, he would need to get tested again. In some cases HIV does not appear until six months after the sexual encounter in question. He didn't have much else to say. I was well aware that he was not looking for false assurances. What he needed at that moment was the presence of another body for nothing other than physical closeness. For the next half an hour he had my entire existence while we sat without speaking.

David was not born into the era of the American AIDS epidemic. Coming of age in the second millennium, he thought of himself as untouchable by the disease that had plagued Americans over two decades ago. David once said that the only time he even thought of himself in relation to the virus was the day he attempted to give blood. The donor eligibility guidelines for the Red Cross state "You should not give blood if you have done something that puts you at risk for becoming infected with HIV." The list of risk activities includes "being a male who has had sexual contact with an-other male, even once, since 1977." The results for the rapid HIV test are available in twenty minutes.

When I visualize David waiting for his results, I picture him naked and sitting upright on the examining table. The examination room is bare, the floors sterile and marble. After a few minutes he crosses one leg over the other, and the paper underneath him crunches and crinkles. Immediately reverting back to legs uncrossed, he notices that his eyes are dry. He must not have been blinking. Exactly twenty-one minutes later, the nurse enters the room and tells him that the test results are negative. She says, "See you again in two months. We'll know for sure then." She leaves the room. He lies down on the table, still naked and breathing heavily, staring at the linoleum ceiling. In actuality, David never took off his clothing. He also said the examination room was warm, as was the nurse. His mother had accompanied him and waited outside in the waiting room.

When David explained to her the situation her reaction was, "Well, you either have it or you don't." She was neither pale nor shaking when her son reentered the waiting room and announced his results. She hugged him. "Almost there," she said. David would have stayed home and in bed that weekend, but his mother reminded him that he had better things to do.

One week later David asked me over to watch the movie version of one of our favorite books, Milan Kundera's *The Unbearable Lightness of Being.*

David always said he longed to be the weightless and free Sabina but he was really the weighted and heavy Teresa at heart. At times, I would glance over at him and notice that he wasn't looking at the screen, but through it. Once or twice

I felt him glancing at me. After the movie ended David asked me, "How much time do you have?" Without really thinking I answered, "Enough." David paused. "Does everybody?" It wasn't a weak question. He was not looking for anything but my honest opinion. "I think so."

Summer had begun making its approach on New England. I made an impromptu visit to David on a Sunday. He was standing on his porch, leaning forward on the railing. I am sure he saw me before I saw him. His eyes followed me as I approached, and before I even reached the stairs he announced, "I'm in love."

"With whom?" "A boy with an eyebrow ring and bright eyes. He walked past me twice today."

David described him further to see if I could pin a name to his mystery prospect. After some speculation and some witty banter, David and I gave up on our detective work. He took off his shirt and suggested we lie out and tan. I flattered him by telling him that it looked as if he had been working out. With a modest smile, he jokingly flexed his biceps.

It didn't occur to me until later that day that the old coffee can and the tobacco graveyard in the front lawn had both vanished. I quit smoking that Monday. The revelations that had made an impact on David resonated in me.

His health was not the only aspect of his life that was endangered by the threat of HIV. David's worldview, as well as mine and his mother's, was altered as a false sense of invincibility was shattered. David began considering his decisions and his actions in terms of their effects on his lifespan. A cigarette was perhaps three fewer minutes of life, whereas a jog around the track was an hour more.

For the first time in his life, David reconciled the idea of strength in numbers with individuality. Asking for the support of others, such as his mother and me, did not make him feel weak, as he had once expected it would. Through disclosure and vulnerability grew strength and a sense of self. He no longer wished for people to be faceless and inaccessible. He was connected to time, people, and himself. In spite of the burdens he carried, his newly deconstructed and then reformed worldview made him feel weightless.

On May 14, David's mother once again accompanied him to the clinic. This time I visualized David jogging into the examination room. He had on athletic shoes and a sweatband around his forehead. He did not sit while waiting for his results. When the nurse came in to give him the results she prefaced it with, "Congratulations." David smiled, warmly, said goodbye and thank you, and left the room the same man he was twenty-one minutes earlier. My imagination is accurate minus the apparel. David later told me that when he delivered the news to his waiting mother, she hugged him close and then slapped him on the back of the head. He was gripped with emotion when he realized how well he understood his mother.

David now runs three miles a day and, as it turns out, the boy with the eyebrow ring is named Kevin. Apparently he was just waiting for David to see him.

Last Call

Openings can come from the bottom up

Laura College

As told by Alan Cade

DEPRESSION IS A condition that most people don't understand. It isn't just an emotional state—it's a disease that infects both your body and your mind. Although the physical symptoms of depression are often subtle, its effects are profound. When I was twenty-six, my lucrative career as a real estate agent and broker went down the tubes, and so began my personal experience with depression.

While bourbon had once been a beverage that I casually enjoyed at cocktail parties and open houses, it suddenly became a constant companion. Rather than devoting my energy to finding a new job and taking care of my wife and two daughters, I turned instead to the bottle for comfort. Alcoholism didn't run in my family, nor had I previously displayed any symptoms. One day I just started drinking, and I couldn't seem to make myself stop.

If you've ever looked for a job while nursing a hangover, then you probably know how much progress I made with my job hunt. I drank myself into a stupor every afternoon and then fell into bed beside my wife when I could no longer keep my eyes open. Our savings began to dwindle, and I'm sure my wife entertained thoughts of leaving me. The depression sunk its teeth into my resolve, and I resigned myself to the notion that it would simply never let go.

On December 18, 1999, I polished off nearly an entire bottle of Wild Turkey while lying on the couch and watching the Game Show network. I recall very little of that afternoon, but I do remember thinking that if I happened to pass out, I might never wake up again. The thought should have terrified me, but instead I was comforted by the idea of never-ending sleep, just as an infant is calmed by his mother's voice. I'm ashamed to say that I wasn't thinking about my wife or my daughters; I was consumed by the thought of my failure to find a job and provide for my family.

I must have passed out between four and five o'clock because I vaguely remember watching *The Price Is Right*. When I finally regained consciousness, I was lying in a hospital bed, staring up at the acoustic-tile ceiling through a haze of fluorescent light and alcoholic incoherence. My wife was sitting at my bedside with her hands wrapped around my wrist, but I lacked the energy to turn and face her.

My wife had found me six hours earlier when she got home from work. I was lying unconscious on the couch with a puddle of vomit on the carpet beside me. She called an ambulance immediately, and I was rushed to the hospital while the paramedics tried unsuccessfully to bring me back to consciousness.

My blood-alcohol level was 0.41 percent, and I had very little response to pain stimulus. The doctors diagnosed me with alcohol poisoning.

The fact that I was still slightly drunk when I came to shocked me to my very core. The doctors refused to release me in that condition, so I stayed in the hospital overnight. Even though our daughters were safe with a neighbor, I insisted that my wife go home. I now realize that I was punishing myself by pushing her away. What right did I have to my wife's companionship when I couldn't take care of myself? And why should she have to settle for this cold, haunted shell of the man I once was?

That night, a nurse named Patsy stopped by my room to check my vital signs. She was a plump woman, pleasantly round with grandmotherly features and a smile that could light up the dimmest corner. She saw the miserable expression on my face and pulled a chair next to the bed, somehow sensing my need to talk.

I told her about the previous few months of my life. I described my descent into depression and alcoholism. "I really didn't think I was doing anything wrong," I told her as tears rolled down my face. "How does a person get to be so stupid?"

Patsy's fingers were cool and firm in my hand as she told me about her experience with alcoholism. Her husband, Roger, had passed away ten years ago from acute liver failure, after spending nearly five years in alcoholic oblivion. "He was always the strong one," she told me, "so I didn't know how to take charge of his life for him. The minute he turned to drink, he started to die, and I didn't do anything to stop it."

I listened with morbid fascination as she described her late husband and his slow, pitiful death. As I listened to Patsy's sad story, it dawned on me that I was too young to give up on life. I imagined what my daughters' lives would be like if they lost their father at such a young age. Patsy asked to see pictures of my kids, so I reached over to my bedside table and tugged them out of my wallet. She looked over the pictures with her kind blue eyes and then taped them to the end of my bed.

"You might not think you owe it to yourself, Alex," she told me, "but you owe it to them."

When I tell this story to friends and family members, they marvel at how quickly I decided to give up alcohol. Of course, they don't realize that there was nothing quick about my recovery, and that every alcoholic's experience is fraught with mistakes and heartaches. Patsy helped me enroll in an Alcoholics Anonymous program the very next morning and, at my request, found a local chapter of Al-Anon for my wife.

Today I spend six months out of every year traveling to high schools in Texas, speaking to students about the dangers of alcoholism. I'm sure that many of those kids see my assemblies as an excuse to skip class, but there are times when my speeches get through, and those few occasions make the effort well worth it.

Patsy was kind enough to take time out of her busy nursing schedule to reach out to me, and hopefully my words sound the last call for someone else going through a similar experience.

Independence Day

How I found the strength
to stand on my own two feet

Elizabeth Anne Hill

As told by Jackie Stone

M Y CHILDHOOD WAS difficult, to say the least. My parents divorced when I was four years old. My father, a severe alcoholic, moved out of the country, leaving my mother and me to fend for ourselves.

My mother was a free spirit who hopped from place to place around the country. She would go wherever she could find work. At least once a year, she would come across a new job opportunity in another city that appeared to be better than the one she had, and off we would go again.

Our nomadic lifestyle insured my place as a perpetual outsider at school. Day in and day out, my greatest concern was finding someone to eat lunch with. There was nothing worse than being the new girl sitting alone at the lunch table. Each day I would find a way to make a new friend, and then I would ask her if I could sit with her at lunch. Somehow I always managed to have someone to sit with.

Outside of school, I didn't have much of a social life. I was never allowed to participate in sports. My mother didn't see the importance of extra-curricular activities. Consequently,

I had no idea what I was good at or what things interested me.

I spent hours daydreaming about having a normal life with friends and activities. At the end of eighth grade, a golden opportunity came to me when my mother decided that she needed to go off to India to find herself. She told me I could go with her or live with my father, who had moved back to California after living in Spain for many years.

I had no intention of going to India. I knew my father was a binge drinker, but I realized that living with him was the only way I could realize my dream of spending all four years of high school in the same place.

The first several months with my father went very well. He was on his best behavior and never touched a drop of alcohol. I developed a tight-knit group of friends at a nearby church group. I was overjoyed and felt as if I was making a fresh start.

Then one day I noticed that my father had begun bringing bottles of wine home from the store. "Dad, I thought you weren't drinking," I pleaded with him. He would always brush me off, saying that he could have a glass or two without a problem.

One day I came home from school and found him passed out on the floor. Frantic, I dialed 911. When the paramedics arrived, they told me he was just drunk and to let him sleep it off. My father had fallen off the wagon, and from that time on his drinking and erratic behavior got steadily worse.

I was tremendously angry inside because I felt that I was playing the role of the parent and my father was acting like a child. It was a heavy burden for a seventeen-year-old girl to bear. I prayed that my father would stop drinking, but he never did.

Going away to college was going to be my saving grace. My father didn't want me to go, but he knew I needed to continue my education and there weren't any colleges I could attend in the area.

In 1984, I was accepted at San Diego State University. My freshman year was the best year of my life. I was sure that I had finally found my way and that everything was going to be all right. But summer break was approaching, and I dreaded going back to live with my father because he was up to his usual antics. He drank constantly and had found a new way to manipulate me: I had a job, so I would have spending money when I returned to college. But every week my father concocted a bill for money he said I owed him. I now had to find a way to pay him so he would allow me to go back to school in the fall.

My second year at college was wonderful, but in the back of my mind was the constant burning question, "What am I going to do for summer break?" I knew there was no way I could endure staying with my father again.

I told my mother of my dilemma, and she suggested spending the summer with my brother in Canada. My brother Bob was nineteen years older than I was, and we hardly knew each other, but I readily agreed to go. Unlike my father, my brother encouraged me to be independent. He sent me a plane ticket and said that I could work in his health club selling memberships twelve hours per day, four days per week. On Fridays I earned my keep by cleaning the entire house and doing the grocery shopping.

To my surprise, I became the top sales person in the health club that summer. It seemed that my years of learning to make friends as I moved around the country had paid off. I knew how to approach people and gain their confidence so that I could recommend they join the gym. The summer was glorious. I made many friends and spent every weekend with my brother and his family touring around Canada.

I was ecstatic because I had earned a total of $1,100 during the summer. It felt so good to make my own money. But on my twentieth birthday I received a letter from my father outlining the money that he said I owed him. It was all of the money I had made for the entire summer. I was devastated. I couldn't imagine working all summer just to hand over my hard-earned money to my father for some imaginary debt.

I sat for hours staring at the letter with tears pouring down my face. Finally, I asked my brother what I should do. He told me, "Well Jackie, you have two options. You can pay him the money and go back to school with his financial support, or you can realize that you can support yourself, as you've done here, and move out on your own."

The thought of venturing out on my own terrified me. "How will I pay all my bills and go to college?" I wondered. But my brother's comments rang in my ears. "You have proven to yourself that you are goal-oriented and strong." I suddenly felt empowered.

I took a deep breath and a leap of faith and made a gut-wrenching choice. I wrote my father and told him that I would not be paying him the money, I would not be living with him, and I was going out on my own. This was a life-changing moment for me. I knew that it wasn't going to be easy, but because of my experience working in my brother's health club, I knew that somehow I was going to find a way to support myself and put myself through school.

Money was extremely tight. All I had was the $1,100 that I had made during the summer. Luckily, I found a friend who needed a roommate, and I decided to attend junior college, which was substantially less expensive than the university. I searched for several weeks for a job and finally was hired as a teller at a credit union and a hostess in a restaurant. I worked seven days per week and fit general education classes in wherever I could.

I wasn't a very good teller. I couldn't seem to balance my drawer and had difficulty with the ten-key calculator. By the end of each day, I had a severe migraine headache from concentrating so hard. I began wearing a large trench coat to work so that I could smuggle the calculator out with me. I spent many late evenings honing my abilities on the calculator. Every day while driving to work, I visualized my mind being sharpened like a knife so that I could absorb as much information as possible. I was extremely motivated to succeed, and I was determined to do what it took to excel at both of my jobs.

Periodically, I met with one of the managers at the credit union to find out what I needed to do in order to be promoted to the next level. Night and day I was consumed with finding ways to improve my skills so that I would become a more valuable employee. I did whatever my supervisors told me I needed to do, and I soon found myself moving steadily up the company ladder until I became the branch manager for the credit union.

For the first time in my life, I knew without a doubt that I was going to be okay and that I had succeeded in my quest to support myself. I quit my restaurant job and attended night school at the University of Phoenix—where with great satisfaction I finished my degree in Management of Information Systems. I continued to excel in my career and held a variety of management positions in large financial institutions.

Looking back, I realize that the difficult decision I made at the age of twenty was the right choice. I gave up all ties to my father and his financial support in order to have control over my own life. I can see now that the challenges I encountered with my mother and father gave me a powerful foundation of inner depth, strength, and courage that has continued to serve me throughout my life.

I never gave up on my goals, and now I have achieved my fondest dream of all. I am a wife and mother in a loving, supportive family. My husband, teenage daughter, sixteen-month-old son, and I work as a team to make our family life run smoothly. I came to the realization that my purpose in life is to pass on my hard-earned wisdom to my children and all others who need a boost of strength to face their own disappointments and challenges.

Funny How Life Works

License to marriage

Amber Gillet

"ALL RIGHT," I groaned. My friend needed a ride to the DMV to renew her license. It was a warm, sunny April day, and the last place I wanted to spend my lunch break was in that small office packed with a lot of other anxious people who wished they were somewhere else too.

We entered the building and scanned the room for open seats. There were two seats available toward the back of the office. As I rounded the corner next to the service desk, a well-built young man caught my eye. He was dressed in a T-shirt and brown jeans. His skin was tanned, and he was dirty from work.

I felt a sting in my stomach as I passed him. Looking back as I walked to my seat, I noticed him glancing in my direction. He rubbed his strong hand across his head and looked at me from under his arm.

I tried to focus on other things. My friend was talking to pass the time, asking questions, but I could manage only one-word answers. Thoughts rushed through my mind. He was going to leave shortly, and it was likely I would never see him again. This was my only opportunity to talk to him. I started to panic; everything around me seemed distant and fuzzy. I

felt disoriented. I decided to get some air outside. I figured
that, at the very least, I might get to see what he was driving
and increase my chances of running into him again.

I walked out and leaned against my car, letting the sun
warm my skin and clear my thoughts. He appeared within
minutes, looked around, and settled down on a brick wall in
front of the building. I was dumbstruck for a minute. This
is what I had hoped would happen, and now I was terrified.
It's funny how life works.

I had two options, and one was to take my chances and
introduce myself. This sounded really stupid now that I was
on the spot, but then I realized that I would never forgive
myself if I didn't act. I let my heart take over, and my feet
started moving.

I introduced myself and explained that I was waiting on a
friend. As we talked, I discovered that he was back in town
after living out of state for several years. He had been rely-
ing on a friend for a ride to work and had finally taken the
time to renew his license. He was a few years younger than
me, but we had grown up in neighboring small towns. We
knew many of the same people but somehow hadn't crossed
paths until now. Seconds later, his ride pulled up. We said
our nice-to-meet-yous and goodbyes, and he walked away
toward the car.

My friend appeared from the building at the same time
he was leaving.

"Did you know him? What are you doing?" she asked.

"Not before today, I didn't. It sounds crazy, but I couldn't
think after I saw him inside. I was hoping I could talk to him
before he left." I suddenly felt silly.

What was I thinking? I had been caught in a moment of dumbstruck attraction. I felt that if I were to see him again, I would have to hide to avoid embarrassment.

"You're nuts," my friend said with a laugh.

We got into my car, and I shifted into reverse. I turned to back out, and there he was, knocking on my window. I jumped and felt my face flush. His friend's car blocked mine in. I rolled down the window and said, "Yes?"

"I was wondering if I could get your number," he asked.

"Okay, but only if you give me yours," I replied. What? Did I just say that? I waited for him to turn and run.

"No problem. Can I use your pen?"

After we exchanged numbers, he smiled and walked away. I needed a minute to regain my bearings. My friend was giggling. "Well, that was crazy!" I looked straight at her and said, "I'm going to marry him and have his kids. He's the one." It sounded as ridiculous coming out of my mouth as everything else I had done in the last hour, but somehow it also made sense.

A year and a half later, I was Mrs. "DMV," and we now have lots of boys and a couple of dogs. Funny how life works.

Where They Belong

Waking up
and smelling the coffee

Joseph Civitella

EDDA WORKED AT a local café as a barista, serving regular coffees, making specialty coffees, and cleaning up tables. She saw many people come and go on a daily basis and eventually got to know most of the regular patrons. Usually in a good mood, she smiled pleasantly, and her laugh was contagious. She made everyone feel welcome in the cafe.

Jessie was a homeless person who hung around by the entrance to the café. She didn't panhandle and was not a nuisance in any "official" sense. Thus the police couldn't intervene to remove her from her spot. When people gave her money, she quietly accepted. When people bought her a coffee or a sandwich, she timidly received the offering and quickly retreated a safe distance away.

When winter set in, Jessie began to make a habit of going into the café to sit wherever she could, usually falling asleep for extended periods of time. Everyone saw her but pretended not to notice. She was dressed in dirty old clothes that were mostly torn, wore old shoes that were falling apart, and her hair was disheveled and in dire need of washing. How she survived from one day to the next was anybody's guess, but the evidence of her homelessness was clearly visible on her face in the form of frostbite.

The café staff didn't mind giving Jessie a free coffee every now and then and perhaps a muffin that might have gone to waste otherwise. As long as Jessie wasn't an annoyance, they let her stay even if some patrons may have considered her a nuisance. She wasn't the kind of customer they wanted, but no one took any action to get rid of her.

The unspoken truce ended one day, though, when Edda witnessed an altercation between Jessie and a regular customer. There were no seats remaining in the café when Wayne entered, and he always sat at a table in order to use his laptop. Edda saw him standing patiently by the main counter when a spot suddenly came free. He approached the couple at the table and asked, "Do you happen to be leaving?"

"Yes, we are," answered the man. "Just as soon as my wife is ready."

"Thank you," replied Wayne.

But unbeknownst to Wayne, Jessie had snuck up behind them and put a plastic bag on the table. When the couple left and Wayne saw Jessie there, he said, "This is my table!"

Jessie retreated a few steps without saying anything. Edda was about to intervene but had to make a chai latté for another customer. Wayne put his briefcase on the table, took a step forward, and faced Jessie. "Why don't you just leave?" he blurted out, loud enough for everyone in the café to hear him.

Jessie withdrew timidly and was not seen again that day. But Edda noticed that Jessie had tears in her eyes as she left the café.

Edda was disturbed by what she witnessed but couldn't confront the customer. It could be construed as bad customer service, and she needed this job. She couldn't really cater to Jessie's needs either because the cafe was not a refuge for the homeless. She wanted to do something because she felt compelled to do so, not because she had to. It was the first time ever that she such a strong call to action.

Edda had planned on forging a career in the café business; she wanted to own her own outlet some day. She had a talent for being able to deal with people, no matter their personality, and that easy disposition would serve her extremely well in business. She also abhorred injustice and unfair treatment. Every person had the right to be cared for, respected, and validated, no matter where he or she was in life or how badly he or she managed to cope. The episode in the café showed Edda that maybe she had to make a positive difference in another way.

Edda ran into Jessie on the streets a few weeks later on a cold and snowy evening. Jessie was huddled against a glass pane in a bus shelter, shivering visibly. The temperature was going to dip well below freezing that night, and Edda knew that this was the kind of night when homeless people were subject to hypothermia. What were Jessie's chances of making it through alive? She already had frostbite on her cheeks.

What about her fingers? Her toes?

No, Edda couldn't just walk away. This is where she decided to draw the line. Maybe people like Wayne could reject Jessie, but Edda couldn't do it. She had to do something to help her.

Edda knelt next to the homeless woman. "Hey, Jessie. Come on, dear. Let me take you home."

But Jessie did not answer.

"Jessie, do you hear me?"

Still she did not answer.

"Either you come home with me, or I'll call 911. You can't stay here tonight."

Jessie didn't move, but she turned her head slightly toward Edda. She just looked at her and didn't say anything.

After trying unsuccessfully to convince Jessie to go home with her, Edda finally decided to call EMS. Within minutes an ambulance arrived. Edda went to the hospital with Jessie and stayed with her until she was admitted.

While in the hospital with Jessie, Edda began to rethink her own life, particularly what she wanted to do. Was running a café the best work she could do? It might be the most profitable, but what about making a more significant contribution to society?

A few weeks later, after much soul-searching, she applied to and was admitted to nursing school. Today, she is in her final year of training and plans to work as a community nurse. She also has kept in touch with Jessie, who eventually received all the health care and social services that she required to get back on her feet. Jessie is now working part-time with Edda in the same café where they first met.

Wayne still comes to the café once in a while and usually finds a free table even if he has to wait. Edda or Jessie serves him his favorite specialty coffee as though he is just any other customer. Because that is what he is regardless of his personal biases. But now Jessie belongs too. No one can tell her,"Why don't you just leave!" And Edda is about to start a new career. She has found where she belonged as well.

Maybe one day Edda or Jessie will tell Wayne how his insensitive behavior toward a homeless person turned two lives around. He was a transient customer who came and went—someone who didn't necessarily belong, at least not in the café or in the lives of Edda and Jessie.

We Are All in the Same Small Boat

The power of words to transform lives

Manette Adams

IN EVERY LIFE there are moments you always remember. I had such a moment in the summer of 1979, when my husband and I visited Israel. On the last day of our vacation, we went to Yad Vashem, the Holocaust Museum that commemorates the six million Jews who died at the hands of the Nazis. The building was simple in design. We joined the line, which moved quietly from one room to another. Each glass case added an emotional impact. In one case, there were piles of eyeglasses. In another, children's shoes, some in pairs. There were books, teeth, bones—all that remained of men, women, and children who died in the genocidal ovens.

Later, as I walked down the exit ramp, blinking in the bright sunlight of the afternoon, I found myself in step with a woman who seemed to be alone. Talking as if to herself, she said softly, "We are doing it again," and there were tears in her eyes. "Now it's the Vietnamese," she added. We exchanged a few words about the "boat people" who were trying to escape life under communism. Even as we spoke, we knew some overloaded fishing boats may be sinking.

Back in Connecticut, I went to the board of deacons at my church with the proposition that our congregation bring a

Vietnamese family to Cheshire. "This may be possible," said one man. "In the fall," another said. A woman added, "In September, we could have a congregational meeting." After we listed the needs of a refugee family on the board, another member suggested my request be put on the next month's agenda. The following day, with my husband's encouragement, I phoned neighbors and friends to attend a special meeting. Their enthusiasm was effusive, and we decided we would move ahead. We had a second meeting and a third. One family offered to put up the refugees in its large family room in the basement until more appropriate housing could be found. Furniture, blankets, children's jackets, pots and pans, toys, and canned goods started coming in.

We easily recruited members for a dozen committees, each with a chairperson. We were getting organized! We would call our endeavor CARE, Cheshire Aids Refugees Effort.

Flash forward two months.

We are at Bradley airport. Harry and I watched nervously as weary passengers filed down the ramp. Last of all, the long-awaited Voong family arrived. First came Chenh, smiling, carrying his dictionary and a beat-up suitcase. Mui, his wife, was several steps behind him. Two youngsters held on to her trousers. She carried the third small boy in her arms. Chenh's younger sister, Denh, emerged last, looking bewildered and clutching a small radio. Later that night, after showing them their new apartment, we offered them rice at their kitchen table. They told us about their journey through pantomime and laughter. With little understanding of how to navigate, they had gotten a small fishing boat. His family and some neighbors brought water and a few supplies, and they headed out to sea.

The weeks and months that followed were full of surprises for our CARE committees and for the Voongs. The Voongs were determined to learn English and to master the telephone, the stove, and the many unfamiliar appliances. Their drive and confidence were awesome, and they were able to make the difficult adjustment to their new life in America. I remember five-year-old Singh's first day of school, when he came home with a big smile on his happy face.

Chenh was thrilled to find a job working at Tudor House, a furniture store in the area. He knew no English and had never seen an upholstering room, but Chenh was a fast learner. A few months later, I bought him a second-hand sewing machine. He immediately offered to cover our couch. He wrote no measurements but spread the fabric out on our basement Ping-Pong table. He picked up the scissors, and we watched breathlessly as he cut. By the end of the day, we realized Chenh would make it in America. The couch was beautiful!

In their first Memorial Day Parade in Cheshire, the Voongs carried a banner that read, "We Love America," along with American flags.

Today, Chenh owns his own upholstery company in Cheshire. His growing family works there, along with a dozen other employees. Chen and Mui's three sons have graduated from UCONN. Their daughter Megan, born in the United States, is now a student at UCONN as well.

The Director of Facilities Management of Whitney Center passed me in the lobby several weeks ago. He called,

"Manette, someone wants to see you." In came Singh Voong, carrying an upholstered chair. I threw my arms around him just as I did in 1980 when he returned from his first day in kindergarten. Later that week, six members of the family came to our apartment with Singh's college sweetheart, Yen Liv, now his wife, and their two small boys. Mui brought a platter of her delicious egg rolls. Singh carried a large, red, newly upholstered chair.

The Voongs are special people. I am privileged to have played a part in their journey. And it all began with a stranger in Israel who shed a tear for the boat people.

The Dancer and the Dance

How I found my calling

Deborah DeNicola

JODY WAS EIGHTEEN years old when she met the celebrated jockey Stanley Dancer. He was two decades her senior, but they enjoyed a wonderfully happy and compatible relationship for forty years. They traveled to famous racetracks around the world and attended prominent races in Hong Kong. They bought horses in New Zealand and rode them along white sandy beaches. Stanley was crowned King of Trotters in Sweden, and he appeared on the Ed Sullivan show with Cardigan Bay, the first harness horse to win a million dollars in prize money. When Stanley was diagnosed with cancer in his seventies, Jody was barely fifty years old. She cared for him at home for seven years until he passed away quietly.

Although she was left with a nest egg, Jody had little experience with taking care of herself, because Stanley had always provided for her and pampered her. She was now alone and surrounded by reminders of Stanley. There were cases full of his trophies, walls draped with commissioned paintings of Stanley and his favorite horses, and photos and plaques hanging all over her oceanside home. She felt bereft and lost, and she found it difficult to put her life in gear.

Months after Stanley's passing, with intense and repeated arm-twisting, Jody's best friends, Frani and BeBe, convinced her to take a weeklong cruise with them to St. Thomas. The cruise line they chose catered to a lively group of ballroom dancing fans and offered five excellent dance hosts and teachers. But Jody, a tomboy in her athletic youth, had to be dragged along by the sleeves of the glittery gowns that her friends convinced her to wear. She reluctantly took lessons in the Argentine tango, waltz, and the challenging paso double.

Jody soon discovered that she had a natural flare for performing. Observing the teachers on that cruise, she began wondering if dancing just might be her thing. One afternoon, as circumstance would have it, she showed up for what she thought was a yoga class, only to find that yoga was not on the schedule. In its place was a class in neuro-integrative-aerobics.

Seeing that NIA was a combination of modern dance, jazz techniques, martial arts moves, tai chi, and yoga, she decided to attend the class out of curiosity. As she began to move, Jody distinctly heard Stan's voice saying, "Darlin', go for it!" And go for it she did. She attended NIA classes three times that week and subsequently registered for a ten-day workshop in Oregon, where NIA originated. She earned her White Belt, certifying her as an instructor.

Within a year of bringing NIA back home with her, Jody became known as the barefoot queen of South Florida. Her natural charisma and talent were the right fit for her community. Jody rented space and set up a business, and she immediately drew both men and women who wanted to tune and tone their bodies while having fun. She taught her students to appreciate their bodies' wealth and beauty, to clarify and clear their minds, and to honor and rejoice in their spirit.

NIA became so popular that Jody developed a workshop to help her students experience their wellness in new and deeper ways. Each class began with a grounding step into a new day and ended with an Asian bow and the universal greeting *Namaste*—"The god in me acknowledges the god in you." The group also formed into a circle, and each student offered something to the universe. Someone would shout, "Gratitude!" Someone else, "Forgiveness!" Then "Bliss!" "Creativity!" "Compassion!" "Peace!" "Sensitivity!" "Love!" Her students continually thanked her for her contagious humor and high energy. She earned her Blue Belt, which allowed her to mentor others, and began thinking about buying her own building, where she could set up mirrored dance studios.

She had settled into a busy, abundant life. Now at age sixty, Jody fully enjoys her active lifestyle. She also travels to dance conferences and makes her own videos. She recently worked her booth at the Whole Heart Expo in the Broward Convention Center. She steadily sold her NIA video and book and happily explained NIA's salubrious benefits. Her technical expertise, medical knowledge, and spiritual approach attracted buyers and fans from all walks of life.

Jody had an exciting life while she was married to Stanley, yet she was always in his shadow. She often commented that he had taken care of her very well, so she willingly cared for him until the end. Still, had she not taken that cruise, had she not mistakenly sought a yoga class on the wrong day, she may never have discovered NIA, her true calling. Perhaps Stanley had arranged it all from the other side. Maybe it was the way her life was meant to go all along. In her spiritual world, she knew there were no accidents. She was the dancer, and her life was the dance.

A Gust of Wind

*A detour that lifted me up
to find my mate*

L.J. Reed

MY LIFE WAS a mess, and I needed to blow off some steam, so one evening right after work, I headed straight for my daughter's house. I was like a whirlwind on the road, blowing right past the familiar landmarks in El Paso. My daughter had a Jacuzzi, and I planned to be in it as soon as possible! The two of us slipped into the hot water, sipped wine, and munched on the supper she had prepared. I couldn't bring myself to get out of the Jacuzzi until after eleven, even though I was due at a client's office the next morning at eight. In an abrupt panic, I threw on some of my clothes, stuffed the rest into my bag and the pockets of my new leather coat, and took off.

The next morning, though a little bent from the wine, I managed to get myself up at the regular time. I took extra care with my appearance because the guy I was going to see could turn out to be an important client. It was November, but the weather was imitating January, so I pulled on my new coat and drove to the client's office.

The moment he saw me, the client gave me a sappy smile, and I felt my self-confidence soar. He asked me to return in the afternoon, however, because he had accidentally made an appointment with one of his own clients for the same time slot.

As I started out the door, his customer came in. That man stepped back and held the door open for me, and I'll be darned if he didn't give me a goofy smile as well. Dang, I didn't know a coat could do that much for a woman. Feeling attractive for the first time in a very long while, I decided to stop in at our biggest client's workplace. I thought it couldn't hurt to breeze through and have him see me looking so fine.

Full of myself, I eventually pranced through our office to the back room, where my partner June was working. She turned her chair toward me to say good morning and burst into helpless laughter. She pointed and shouted through tears of mirth, "I sure hope you didn't have any client appointments this morning!"

I looked down to where June was pointing. Both legs of yesterday's black pantyhose cascaded from the side pocket of my cream-colored leather coat, draping gracefully almost to the hem.

I must admit that it was funny for about three minutes. Then pictures began to scroll through my mind's eye—I saw myself at those clients' offices, thinking I looked so good. And they were laughing at me all the time. I suddenly felt very foolish, and very homely. I guess it's true that the higher you soar, the farther you fall.

When the office phone rang later that morning, I answered with my usual "Hello," but I heard a pathetic catch in my voice.

It was Donna. "Laurie, what's wrong?"

"Ah, nothing. Everything's fine." I liked Donna, but she was not a close enough friend to confide in.

"Okay. Well, listen, Richard and I were talking…"

Richard, a man I'd known since sixth grade, was Donna's boyfriend. He and I grew up together in Van Horn, Texas, and my first husband was best man at his wedding. We seldom saw each other now—our social lives had gone in different directions. Donna explained that Richard had been thinking about me—trying to match me, that is, to his boss, Chuck. Donna said that Richard wondered if it would be all right for him to give Chuck my phone number. According to Richard, Chuck was a very nice man, highly intelligent, my age, good-looking, and unhappy with the kind of women he'd been meeting since his divorce.

"That would be fine, Donna. I'm sure he's nice if Richard says so."

After we hung up, I was furious with myself. Why did I do that? If Chuck was as great as Richard says, then he sure as heck was not going to be interested in me. Oh well, maybe he wouldn't even call.

But Chuck did call me, two hours after I spoke with Donna, while June was out for lunch. His voice was soft, but it still conveyed a managerial tone. He seemed eager—maybe Richard had lied about my looks—yet he didn't utter a single persuasive word. Plainly, he was expecting me to decide whether or not we would meet. He suggested a drink after work.

Despite being tired of the dating scene beyond belief, I heard myself say, "Okay." We set up a time and place—Bennigan's at five o'clock.

The restaurant was three minutes from my office. At five, I convinced myself to go to Bennigan's instead of heading home. After the morning's experience, I couldn't bear the sight of my new leather coat, so I left it on the rack. Instead, I pulled on a brown sweater-jacket that I kept at the office.

When I parked at Bennigan's, the fatigue hit me again. God, I hated this. For two years, I had been dating every kind of man El Paso had to offer... except for the right one. I was already tired from drinking too much wine the previous night and not getting enough sleep. I was weary, to say the least! I backed out of the parking spot and started driving away. But as I veered toward home, I felt my car falter against a strong wind blowing straight at me. For some mysterious reason, nature made me turn the car around. I was going back to Bennigan's.

Walking by the huge picture windows at the front of the restaurant, I saw my reflection. I was a mature forty-five-year-old woman—certainly not a hot young chick.

There I was, wearing an old brown sweater-jacket that looked terrible with my other clothes, my nose already red and dripping from the cold, my long hair pulling out of its clips and flying around my face. Geez, I was so homely! I was sure that when Chuck looked at me, he would think, "Oh man, what have I gotten myself into?" Why the hell was I there anyway, subjecting myself to more disappointment? I whirled around to go back to the car, feeling beaten. But a vicious gust of cold wind hit me in the face, and, without realizing what I was doing, I turned around once more. Bennigan's door was three feet in front of me. Chuck was Richard's friend, I said to myself—his boss, for heaven's sake! I'd promised to meet him, and I was already ten minutes late. I stepped to the door and went inside.

Chuck had been sitting at a booth with a good view of the large windows and the entrance. He had seen me walk by and was rising, coming toward me with his hand extended. I recognized him because he had told me he would be the short guy in the ostrich boots. I hadn't told him what I looked like, so how did he know it was me? Oh, yes, of course, Richard must have given him a description. He wasn't so short after all, but he *was* wearing a gorgeous pair of ostrich boots. He was deep-chested and broad-shouldered. He had salt-and-pepper hair, and he gave me a *great* smile. He did not appear to be wondering what he'd gotten himself into.

As the gusts of wind would have it, we've been married for twenty-four years now, and I haven't felt homely for a moment since I met him. It hasn't even mattered to him if my pantyhose are flailing out of my pockets. Every time I feel wind against my skin now, I remember the most important thing in my life—my husband. What was once a mess has turned into a blessing. The wind sent me into the arms of the right man for me.

I Will Survive

A stranger offers new hope

Sylvia Bright-Green

I ENCOUNTERED MY FIRST angel in 1995, between Christmas Day and New Year's Day, two months after my husband's death.

Sitting in my doctor's waiting room, I succumbed to feelings of hopelessness and despair, and I allowed my tears to escape freely. Losing my husband was devastating enough, but discovering that I was one step away from being a bag lady also took its toll on me.

As I sobbed into my handkerchief, I felt a gentle touch on my shoulder. A stranger stood beside me and asked, "Can I help you?"

"Startled, I stammered, "I... I doubt it. No one in this city or this county can seem to help me. So I don't know what you can do."

"Try me," she said, sitting down next to me. "You just never know."

Through tears of anguish, I poured out my story. I told her about my husband dying a week after we moved to Rhinelander, Wisconsin, and that I lost his work pension because he had inadvertently signed the wrong box on the insurance form. I explained that I wasn't eligible for General Assistance in this county because there was no aid for single people less than sixty years of age. I revealed to her that I didn't qualify for food stamps because my car was valued at more than $2,000. I explained to her that the city's Subsidized Housing Program has a two-year waiting list.

I disclosed that the insurance policy for our car, a bank loan, and a charge card were not going to be paid off, even after making our life insurance payments for months. I explained that I wasn't able to work for five dollars an hour to supplement my Veteran's Administration check of $439 a month because if I did, they would take away my monthly benefit.

"All this and more," I blurted out to the stranger through a stream of tears. "I don't have enough money to pay my $550 monthly rent. If no one else cares that I fall between the cracks in the system, then why should I?"

"I care," replied the stranger, and she grabbed my hand to console me. "I understand your plight, and I know our system leaves a lot to be desired, but…"

Before she could say another word, I put my hand up like a stop sign. "I only have four more months before I'm eligible for a widow's pension, and I can earn up to $8,600 a year in addition to the pension." I wanted her to know that I wasn't seeking a handout.

"Don't worry," she said, squeezing my hand to reassure me. "You will make it. I'm going to see to it that you do."

"But how?" I asked. "No one else, not even the county, churches, organizations, or legislative officials can find me immediate financial assistance."

"I'll show you how," she replied.

She reached into her purse and pulled out a checkbook. "This morning, I asked God, 'How can I best serve you?' Suddenly, I felt an overwhelming desire to come here, even though it's my day off. When I walked into this waiting room and saw you crying, I knew that God had brought us together. Our meeting was no coincidence. Just remember, belief is hanging in there, faith is letting go and letting God take over."

She tore a check from the book and handed it to me. "This is a gift, not a loan. Someday, when you have it, pass it on to whomever God sends onto your path to serve."

As she placed the check in my hand, I thought, "Gosh, I hope she isn't a kook. I can't handle another source of negativity in my life right now."

She took my hand again and said, "All I ask is that you don't tell anyone who I am, because I don't normally go around doing this. And remember, if God has watch over the fields and the animals, then he certainly has watch over you as well."

She gave me a hug and walked away.

I reached into my pocket to retrieve the check on the way to my car after my doctor's appointment. I wanted to read the name of my benefactor and see if she was genuine. Even if she wasn't, I knew that it didn't matter. She had restored my belief that when we focus on what is missing in our lives, we are blind to our present blessings. I also had to admit that after my encounter with her, I experienced a heightened sense of awareness that I would be all right and that a *"presence"* was taking care of me.

Reveling in the feeling of hope, I voiced aloud, "Thank you, God, for renewing my faith. I know I will make it. I promised my husband that I would survive, and I will."

I then glanced down at the check in my hand and noticed the name. My benefactor was a doctor at the clinic, and she had given me a thousand dollars.

Today, eleven years later, I am able to pass her gift on to many others, in smaller denominations. From an angel came a blessing that helped me become an angel myself. I survived, and now I am helping others to survive.

Ruth and the Rabbi

How I found my family

Bethany Garfield
As told by Ruth Gross

IMAGINE A WORLD with no past. This was the reality I experienced for most of my life. As a little girl, there were no pictures of my grandparents on the mantle, nor any keepsakes to hold onto while my mom told me stories about life as a child. Growing up, I always felt a little empty, never knowing what it was like to have cousins to play with or an uncle who looked a little like Dad. My past was somewhat intangible, almost as though it were filled with ghosts.

I was born in 1946, a year and a half after the liberation of Auschwitz (where my father had been for four years), at a Displaced Persons Camp. Located in Salzburg, Austria, this was the camp where my parents first saw each other. I've always said that my parents wouldn't have met had it not been for the war, because they came from different ends of Poland, so, to me, that encounter in itself is a miracle.

After my parents and I spent two and a half years in the DP camp, my great-uncle brought us to the United States, where we settled in the Lower East Side of Manhattan. My father owned a fruit store. My mother, who had a better grasp of the English language, worked the counter.

While both of my parents were prisoners of the Nazis during World War II, they spoke very little of it. There was never a past. With my parents, it was always forward. It wasn't until I was thirty-one years old, with a daughter of my own, that my mother finally spoke about the past. It took a grammar school research project for my daughter to bring out the truth about what had happened.

I always wondered about my family—for example, who my grandmother on my mother's side had been, what she looked like, and whether or not there were people out there, somewhere, who looked like me and shared a similar background. I did not discover the answers to these questions for almost fifty years, despite spending much time searching the Internet for the Halisiewicz genealogy and seeking information from organizations dedicated to putting families of Holocaust survivors back together.

In February of 2005, I was offered the opportunity to escort a friend as an aide to the March of the Living in Auschwitz/Birkenau, Poland. March of the Living is a program that takes place each year, in which thousands of participants take part in a walk to honor the lives lost during the Death March of World War II. The March took place on May 5, 2005—the sixtieth anniversary of the liberation of Auschwitz.

I was eager to go to Poland, as my father had been a prisoner there. It was important to make the connection and reconcile myself with who I am and from where I came. Little did I know, however, that this trip would mark a new connection with my past that I had been searching for my whole life.

There were many moving moments during that trip to Poland. I remember exiting the plane after landing in Warsaw and seeing a rabbi praying. He was actually praying in Poland. It was fascinating to me that Jews were now openly praying where they once could not. I attended a ceremony at a crematorium in Birkenau. I broke down at that point—to touch the walls where somebody had once scraped really affected me.

But, it wasn't until the day of the march that I experienced the most important moment of the journey. It was a gray, rainy day, and the only light came from the candles people were holding as they walked a mile of railroad to Auschwitz. There were 18,000 people marching in silence, each one carrying a wooden plaque. On each plaque was written the name and hometown of family members lost during the Holocaust.

While walking through the crowd, an old friend of mine, Rabbi Benjamin, approached me and said something rather peculiar. "Thank you for picking up my plaque," he said. The rabbi assumed it had fallen from his pocket while marching and was grateful that I had found it.

I looked down at the plaque in my hand and then looked back at him. "What do you mean? This is my plaque." We conversed briefly about the names on each plaque, and within moments it became clear that my mother and the rabbi's father-in-law may have been first cousins.

The rabbi looked at me, stunned. He turned white and then walked away to the head of the crowd. My family name, Halisiewicz, is not a common one. I knew that something amazing had just happened. I think we both understood, and I think the people around us also understood what was happening. He continued on because I think he had to digest it.

Rabbi Benjamin and I had found a connection. After questioning the rabbi later, and realizing that both my family and his wife's family had multiple sets of twins in their ancestries, I felt certain that the discovery was more than just a coincidence. Many people in the crowd noticed the same thing, and soon the word had spread. "Did you hear about the cousins who found each other?" I left Poland knowing that my life had been changed forever. When I returned to the states, Rabbi Benjamin's wife put me in touch with her brother, Jeff, who had been researching the family line for years.

After some comparison of the data that we had both gathered, Jeff and I discovered that our respective grandfathers were brothers. Jeff had been trying to piece together the entire family history for some time but had been unable to find information on the last brother in their grandfather's family.

There was one brother who had been missing. There was one line that they couldn't get any information on, and, incredibly, that was my line.

Since making contact with the rabbi and his family, I have found photographs of my mother's family and other people who resemble her, who unfortunately passed away before the discovery. Jeff has also provided me with additional information about the family, including a list of birth and death records from my mom's hometown. I have been able to figure out when my grandmother died and when her mother was born. All my life, I thought my mother was the last of her family line. But this trip, with the intersection of our paths and our reuniting, gave me back a living family that I never knew existed.

I have been seeking that "living family" in order to recreate my world, with a past I can touch. The Nazis did not wipe out my entire family. I finally have something tangible to dispel the ghosts with. I now have what I always sought—a link from my past to my future.

Running Home

A family recovers from alcoholism

Leslie Galiker

NEW YORK CITY, 1954: The weather that evening was perfect. Gone were the gusty winds that had swirled during March and the persistent rain that had riddled the city streets in April. May had a sweet smell, Gerry thought, as she walked through the East Side streets of Manhattan with her mother that evening. Some of her school friends were playing Double Dutch, expending all their energy before being called in to dinner. Gerry and her mom moved apart to let roller skaters zoom from the sidewalk onto the street. Gerry felt so happy; the smile wouldn't leave her face. Her mom looked really good, much prettier than some of her friends' mothers. And Gerry knew that not many of her friends would be going out to dinner that night. They would be eating at home. Her mother wanted alone time with Gerry, she had told her, time away from Grandma and Grandpa.

Gerry lengthened her stride to match that of her mother. At this rate, they would be at The Gables, way over on the West Side, in no time.

A few weeks ago, on her eleventh birthday, Gerry had made her mom promise. "I can stop anytime," her mom had laughed. "I don't even like the stuff," she added. After a lot of pleading, her mom promised Gerry that, yes, she would stop drinking. Mom just wasn't the same when she drank. She had kept her word so far, coming straight home after work. Tonight was their first night dining out; this would be the test.

Finally, they reached The Gables. This was the very best, her favorite of all Italian restaurants. It was nothing special, really. There were red-and-white-checked tablecloths that one finds in many Italian restaurants, but the waiters were really cute. They paid attention to what Gerry had to say, the food was delicious, and the families at other tables always seemed to look so happy.

Gerry was surprised when her mom motioned to the waiter so quickly. They hadn't even opened their menus.

Before her mother even spoke to the waiter, Gerry knew what she was going to say. "A dry martini, please, with a twist of lemon." Her mom turned a bright smile onto Gerry. "Don't worry...I promised, remember? I'll be good." To Gerry, the promise had to do with not drinking at all. Or hadn't she made that clear to her mother?

The veal scallopini was delicious, as usual. Gerry had developed tastes in food that many of her friends didn't have, basically because she and her mother dined out often. She never ordered spaghetti and meatballs, because no one could make them as well as her mom did. Now, Gerry felt a familiar uneasiness rolling around, giving her the start of stomach pains. She pushed the food around her plate not able to eat any more.

Her mother drained her second martini. Gerry heard, but wasn't really listening, as her mother spoke of this and that.

All Gerry knew was that mom's voice was rising. A familiar pattern was being played out once more. To add to her growing stomach pains, Gerry felt her face flushing with embarrassment. She knew this was true: some people really must have eyes in the backs of their heads. She certainly felt that she did, because Gerry just knew that some of the restaurant's customers were now staring at her table; the room was much quieter than it had been minutes ago.

As her mother planned their weekend, Gerry heard slurred words. She saw unfocused eyes. "It's okay, honey, I feel fine," her mother said to her. But Gerry didn't feel fine. Gerry felt her heart drop to the pit of her stomach as her mom brought the cocktail glass down from her lips to place it on the table, and it missed and crashed to the floor. Gerry suddenly knew she just couldn't take this any more!

Without a word to her mother, and not daring to meet anyone's eyes, Gerry jumped up from her seat. She carefully yet quickly ran around the tables and out of the restaurant, into the now-darkening world of Manhattan at night.

Tears blurred her vision as Gerry ran across avenues and along the street. The lump in her throat felt like a rock, stuck there. She received no incredulous looks, just curious acceptance, typical of New Yorkers.

Everyone was basically in his own world, and this allowed Gerry, at such a young age, to run the streets without question and without being stopped. She was relieved that she didn't encounter anyone she knew.

A childhood of climbing trees, doing endless cartwheels, and jumping rather than walking made it easy to navigate

from the West Side to the East Side. Gerry recalled her
mother's last big binge. She remembered wondering if her
mom would ever stop throwing up. She remembered the loud
snoring as her mother passed out on the couch, naked. Gerry
hid behind her bedroom door, not daring to come out, but
saw through a crack her grandmother silently covering her
adult child with a warm blanket. Why? Gerry would ask her
mother. Her mother would just shake her head with a puzzled
look on her face when Gerry questioned her drinking. Gerry
stopped asking.

It was almost completely dark when Gerry reached her
apartment. Some Puerto Rican neighbors were sitting on
the stoop next door, softly singing songs from their country.
Gerry always liked to hear that. Now she just dashed to her
grandmother and grandfather. She couldn't talk, she was
sobbing so much. Her grandmother nodded her head. A
knowing look passed between her grandparents. They knew
why she was alone, and surmised what had happened. Not
long after her arrival home, Gerry heard the sound of a taxi
stopping in front of the building. An unsteady click of heels
sounded in the hallway. A loud bang shook the floor. Her
grandfather flung open the apartment door and went to help
Gerry's mother, who had fallen.

"Gerry, talk to me," her mother said, as she entered the
apartment and pushed her father's arms from her. Gerry ran
to the little room and hid behind boxes stored there. Now the
rock that she had felt in her throat was a boulder.

Weeks later, the lump long disappeared, Gerry searched
one day for the diary where she daily put her most personal

thoughts. She found it under her mom's pillow. Also under a pillow was a newspaper advertisement about Al-Anon and Al-A-Teen. Without discussing why, Gerry asked her mom to take her to an Al-A-Teen meeting, then another. Gerry's mom agreed. One day, when she came home from school, she found her mother home from work early. Gerry's heart dropped as she saw her mother head for the door. Her mom went to her, and took Gerry's face in her hands. "I am going to an AA meeting. I am going to get better."

Time passed. They both went to their meetings. Alcoholism was a disease, her mom learned. There were slips. But they were few. How did this affect Gerry? She was finally able to gain weight. Her grades began to rise. Finally, Gerry could invite friends over to her apartment without worry. And—this is what Gerry felt best about—she mustered up the courage to speak to a little girl in her neighborhood whom she knew was going through the same problems; her mother was also an alcoholic. Gerry told her story, the little girl listened, and Gerry saw hope replace fear in her eyes.

Fish or Chips

Call me lucky—I lost a fortune

Arnold Carmel

IT WAS SEPTEMBER 1965. My wife and I had just departed from Israel, where we lived for five years on a kibbutz. Serving as volunteers in the socialist experiment known as a kibbutz, though fascinating and gratifying, was not a very lucrative endeavor. We left the kibbutz without a nickel in our pockets and took up residence with my parents in London, my birthplace.

My wife, Judy, was quickly employed as a secretary in a paper company in central London, and I worked nights on a production line, putting filaments into lightbulbs. It was not the most stimulating type of work, but, hey, we were just starting out. I would return exhausted early in the morning and fall into bed, just as Judy was waking up to start her day. We hardly had time to talk!

After sleeping six hours, I would wake and begin to study, as I was taking three different correspondence courses in order to complete my high school education. These activities were all that comprised my life at that time, except for one important item. Each week, I filled out the "soccer pool." In England, there are five soccer divisions, with approximately thirty teams in each division. Like many sports gambling games, you predicted the outcomes of the games in order to win. However, the odds of winning anything were slim to none. Like many others, I survived the daily grind and lived for the day when I would win it big and my life would take an entirely new direction. I wanted to own a fish and chips bar! Each week, I handed Judy my form and asked her to purchase a money order and send it to the soccer pool company.

One weekend, while checking the results of the soccer pools, my heart skipped a beat. I realized that I had predicted most of the wins, and my form had a payout of over 50,000 pounds ($150,000 forty years ago!). After telling my mother, I sat alone with this news until Judy returned home that evening. Well, actually I couldn't sit, so I paced our tiny room, bubbling with anxious enthusiasm and dreams of plenty. When Judy walked in, I maintained my composure and casually asked her, "Judy, did you send in the pools?" "I think so," she said nonchalantly, as she went to her purse and pulled out the form. "I guess I must have forgotten." She did not know what that pool form would have meant for us, and I swore my mother to secrecy.

Five months later we had saved enough money to purchase tickets on the Lykes Shipping Line from Liverpool, and we docked in New Orleans after traveling for three weeks. We took a bus to Houston, where I enrolled to get an undergraduate degree at the University of Houston. I went on to get a doctorate in school psychology, and ever since I have worked with kids of all ages in many different environments. My career of more than forty years as an educator has brought me riches beyond anything I could have imagined when I was working the night shift—or for that matter, when I was immersed for those three exciting hours in my grandiose visions of what we would do with $150,000. I have seen shy children with bright ideas emerge into community leaders. I have nurtured kernels of social justice in kids who would go on to make major contributions to society. In some small way, I feel I have done much more than I ever could have as the owner of a fish and chips bar. I have helped feed some of the minds of the future students I hope and believe will have an impact on the world.

Not long after I received my doctorate, Judy and I got into a little tiff, and in response to something she said, I exploded: "Well, it certainly is not as ridiculous as forgetting to send in a soccer form that was worth 50,000 pounds!" Not believing me, she called my mother to confirm that I was not spinning a yarn. But I had kept the form and the result page; I had held on to them over all these years!

I could not be more grateful for the twist of fate that not winning allowed me, the *thin thread* that propelled me to push myself in another direction and make my life what I wanted it to be. Had we actually won the money, no doubt we would have gone into the fish and chips business, and I never would have discovered my true calling in life!

Where Is My Bag?

When bad fortunes
turn out to be good fortunes

Peter Victor

PETER WAS TIRED and lonely. He was a long way from his home in beloved New England. He had flown to Houston, Texas, to seek work as a merchant marine. He was young, new to shipping, and a little scared. He came from a big, loving family and wasn't used to the cold, passionless faces that surrounded him. Nobody in the union hall would acknowledge his presence, and he wished very much that he were not alone. Peter looked at the shipping board, and felt a cold and electric tension as the dispatcher began putting up jobs. One ship caught his eye—the *SS Poet*. Attached to this ship was one job for an officers' messman. This was a person who picked up the dishes after the officers ate their meals. In days of old, this person was called a *cabin boy*. Peter slowly and tentatively wove his way through the older men and threw his shipping card on the table. "You want this job, son?" The dispatcher looked at the card and then looked at Peter.

"Yes sir." Peter's voice sounded small.

"Then you have it. Make sure you get to Galveston on time. I will have your paperwork in a minute." Minutes later Peter stepped out into bright, sunlight and began walking toward the bus terminal.

The heat seeped into the bus station. Peter could feel his shirt beginning to stick to his back. He held a five-dollar bill in his hand. He was almost out of money. Peter calculated that after lunch and after the bus ride to Galveston, he would have about three dollars left. This was fine as long as he could get onboard the ship.

"Where to?" The bus station attendant asked.

"Galveston." Peter's voice again sounded small. The attendant did not answer, and Peter wondered if he had heard him. He was preparing to repeat himself when the attendant's hand appeared before his face.

"That will be three dollars and seventy-five cents; the bus leaves at two thirty. Be here ten minutes early," he said.

"Yes, sir. Can I check my bag? I want to get something to eat before I leave." The hand was extended again. After a brief moment of confusion, Peter handed over his bag and turned to leave.

"You're going to need this baggage claim, son." Peter turned and took the stub of paper, crossed the floor of brown tile, and stepped outside.

Heat rose in waves from the shimmering metal. The tires pounded the dry scarred concrete, making a dull moan that provided the backdrop to Peter's thoughts. He was slumped in his seat by the window. A young woman sat in the front seat beside the driver. She gently consoled a small child. Across the aisle sat an elderly man with a dirty white sailor's hat and a scraggly beard; his head was turned toward the opposite window. A young man with greasy hair and bloodshot eyes nervously paced up and down the aisle, occasionally shooting a glance at one of the passengers. The driver watched him in his mirror. All were quiet. The bus moved down the highway towards Galveston. The brakes made a large squeal, and the doors of the bus slammed open. The woman in front scooped up her child, picked up her bag, and exited the bus. Slowly and in single file, the rest of the passengers followed her. Peter stepped out and the wind ruffled his hair. The oppressive heat of Houston had been replaced by a soft breeze tinged with salt.

Peter had always loved the ocean and was glad to be near it now. The driver slowly lifted the baggage compartment door. One by one, he threw the bags on the ground beside the bus. A small cloud of dust rose as the last bag fell. Peter looked at the empty compartment and then at the driver. "Where is my bag?" he asked.

"I don't know, son. If you have a baggage claim, see the guy inside. I don't know why your bag was not put on the bus, but we'll get it here." Peter was filled with anxiety. He was supposed to be on the ship, but he could not go without his bag. To depart on a sea voyage without gear was unthinkable.

Two hours had passed since he had arrived in Galveston. Several phone calls had been placed to the Houston terminal. They had assured Peter that they had his bag, and that it would arrive on the next bus. Yet three more buses had arrived without Peter's gear. "Can you call them again?" Peter asked the terminal agent.

"I have called them several times son—your bag is coming." Another two and a-half hours passed, and it was dark outside. By this time Peter was nearly five hours late for his job.

A driver entered the terminal carrying Peter's bag. Peter grabbed it from his hand and was through the door. Ten minutes later he was walking up the gangway to the ship. He saw the captain watching him approach. Seconds later he stood in front of the captain. The captain held his hands open. "I am sorry, but we have a guy here. I don't know how it happened, but I cannot pay two people. I am sorry, son. You'll have to leave." The captain walked away, and Peter turned to go down the gangway.

"Hey, come here a second," a voice said. Peter had been halfway down the gangway when he heard the hailing. He turned and saw a crewmember beckon him. "You don't want to be walking around down there at night with a bag on your shoulders. My partner has gone home for the night, so you can sleep on his rack. Tomorrow morning after breakfast, we'll pass the hat, so you'll have money to return to Houston."

Peter recalled this kind gesture. He recalled the strange circumstances surrounding his lost bag and the person who'd been sent to fill a job that he had taken. During the next fifteen years, he had never seen that happen again. He recalled the crewmembers going into their pockets at the breakfast table and handing him money. He recalled his trip back to Houston and how he had uneventfully joined a ship called the *Overseas Valdez*. He will always remember sitting at the breakfast table of the *Valdez* months later at sea. The captain had walked in and put up a notice: "*SS Poet*, RIP." Peter had turned to the crewmember next to him and asked, "What's RIP mean?" The sailor stared at him quizzically.

"Rest in peace," said the sailor.

Peter remembered how the *SS Poet* became a mystery. It had vanished without a trace. There had never been a distress call, and one of the largest air and sea searches failed to uncover a trace of the ship, crew, or cargo.

Twenty-four years have passed since the *SS Poet* was lost. Peter's young son Eliott charges Peter and throws his arms around him. Peter remembers the phone call from his sister years earlier. "Whether you know it or not, that was divine intervention," she said. Peter wonders about his mission and why he did not sail with the *SS Poet* that day. He thinks of the kindness of the crew.

"Papa, can you play for a while?" Peter's ten-year-old son, Luc, asks. Peter had ceased shipping when Luc was born.

"Only for a little while, Luc; then I have to go inside and write a bit." Peter's eyes are moist with recollection. He gently picks up Eliott and walks toward Luc. Peter does not know what is expected of him. But he does know that he owes what he was given—love and kindness—every day to every person. From this strong foundation, he strives to build "good" days. He hands the glove to Eliott, and throws the ball to Luc while smiling. The sun is warm and pleasant, and the beautiful day is truly a gift.

The above events occurred as written. Peter J. Victor shipped with the United States Merchant Marine from 1980 to 1994.

He was shipped to the SS Poet in Galveston on March 18, 1980, and shipped on the Valdez the following day. He now lives in Ellsworth, Maine, with his wife and two sons. No trace of the Poet was ever found.

Unforeseen Turn

Turning an obstacle into invention

Kate Kowsh

H E KNEW HIS ribs were broken because he could taste iron from the blood in his mouth. After tumbling over the handlebars of his Suzuki GSXR1000 motorcycle, twenty-five-year-old Jeremy McGhee's body grated against the pavement, skidding to a ragged halt in the middle of a busy California intersection. For the first time in his life, he couldn't feel or move his legs. He lay there, stunned by the hard landing, taking stock of his injuries. As Jeremy's thoughts cleared, he began contemplating a question that had never occurred to him before—What would life be like without the use of his legs?

Jeremy had been an active young adrenaline junky who balked at the thought of sitting still. With this accident, his fate took an abrupt twist, and he would soon discover that he'd spend each day of the rest of his life writing his own answer to that grim question.

His body sprawled across the hot asphalt road and bleeding internally, the thread of Jeremy's life stretched almost to the point of snapping. Looking back, he considers it pure chance that a pair of on-duty paramedics were catching a quick lunch across the street. After watching the carnage unfold, they dropped their food and ran over to him.

Later at the hospital, when doctors huddled around to inform Jeremy of the extent and severity of his injuries, he already knew. Jeremy was trained in first aid and emergency response as a lifeguard, so he understood the nature of his injuries.

During the month and a half he spent recovering from the spinal cord injury that left him a paraplegic, Jeremy waded through the sludge of uncertainties that accompany the kind of news that chances were slim he'd ever walk again. While struggling to stay afloat in this emotional tidal wave, he found himself being called on to make logistical, level-headed decisions about things he had never thought about before. For instance, he had to choose the best type of wheelchair for his active lifestyle and learn to file insurance claims correctly. In the meantime, a mountain of medical bills began piling up. But, even as he lay in his hospital bed, fighting the windfall of new challenges suddenly set in his path, Jeremy knew that he still had control over his life.

He found himself at a crossroads. He could accept his life as it was and move forward, or he could wallow in misery over what had happened to him. Jeremy didn't allow himself to see the glass as half empty for long. Although he couldn't control whether his legs would allow him to walk again, he knew he could control how he dealt with his current condition. Wheelchair or no wheelchair, Jeremy wasn't one to lie down, even after he'd been knocked pretty hard. As he'd soon discover, though, there's no instruction manual for teaching people how to adjust when piecing a wheelchair into the equation of their lives. Although he had friends and family around him to offer support, they knew as much about living with this type of disability as he did—nothing.

It was during his recuperation time in the hospital, that the wheels started turning for Jeremy. As he attempted to reclaim his life, he began to see the need for an organization to help people get back on their feet, both figuratively and literally.

Enter Fight2walk, the non-profit organization that Jeremy founded to mentor those facing spinal cord injuries. Instead of looking at his injury as a burden, he chose to offer himself as a living example that, although life doesn't always go as expected, it doesn't mean you can't continue to live. The day he was discharged from the hospital, using a car with specially adapted hand controls, Jeremy drove himself to the Rocky Mountains in Colorado to spend some time skiing and getting on with his life's journey. In the six years since his accident, Jeremy hasn't stopped pushing the limits of the human spirit.

These days, Jeremy mentors others facing spinal cord injuries, helping them combat the claustrophobia that he says is one of the toughest challenges of paralysis. They don't call it "confined to a wheelchair" for nothing. As part of his non-profit, Jeremy also raises funds to buy adapted sporting equipment such as hand-control bicycles and adapted ski chairs. Jeremy says that he's trained himself to pull through the bad days by thinking about the incredible people he's met on his journey—people whose challenges far surpass his own. This helps Jeremy feel thankful for all he does have.

Jeremy works as a seasonal ski instructor on California's Mammoth Mountain, using a single ski and an adapted ski chair. He teaches others with disabilities how to overcome the claustrophobia of paralysis by getting outdoors. His pursuits at pushing the limits were even featured in the ski video *One: A Lucid Experience*, which chronicled his gargantuan seventy-foot ski jump.

As Jeremy later learned, spreading awareness that people can overcome great adversity isn't accomplished only through monumental feats. In an enlightening ray of irony, the day after he successfully completed his epic ski jump, Jeremy rolled into a local bank to cash a paycheck, and a sweet old lady struggled to open the door for *him*. Jeremy grabbed the door and smiled at her show of kindness. He waved her in and said, "Nope, ladies first." Jeremy realized the small gestures sometimes speak as loudly as the larger ones.

As his story continues, Jeremy humbly assumes his role as mentor and champion for a cause he never imagined himself a part of. He'll always remain conscious of the fact that one unforeseen turn of events has brought him to an apex of human existence he could never have imagined, a place where he chooses to use his experiences—bad and good—to help others.

Jumping the Fence

*You never know
what's on the other side of tomorrow*

Lisa Arneth

A T THE AGE of twenty-two, I believed that I had *arrived*! I had managed to graduate from college, had a fairly good job as a Human Resources assistant, and had recently freed myself from a difficult relationship. I had a degree, was employed, single, and loving it. I was able to pay my bills on time for a change, and I was finally able to feed my cats name-brand cat food instead of the somewhat dicey "no frills" brand. They too were enjoying my newfound success. Although I had money in the bank for the first time in my life, I was still a newbie when it came to financial security. My long-honed skills at saving a buck whenever and wherever possible were in evidence the night I met my husband.

It was a great summer night, one of the last evenings in August. My girlfriend and I had heard about a new bar, built next to a small municipal airport. The takeoffs and landings of the single-engine Cessnas and Piper Cubs added to the atmosphere. The grounds of the restaurant had fire pits out back, bordering the runway, and groups of young twenty-somethings sat around talking, laughing, and enjoying the balmy night. There was one drawback, however—a five-dollar cover charge at the front door. Mary and I were opposed to paying money to walk into a bar, just so that we could pay even more money for drinks. So we decided to take a walk around back to see if we could slip in unnoticed.

There was a small split-rail fence to block the entry of cheapskates like us. It was so short that it almost invited you to hop over and get in for free. Well, at least that's the way we saw it. So, up and over we went, trying desperately to seem nonchalant and be inconspicuous.

Mary went first, and I quickly followed. No sooner had my feet touched the ground than a group of guys started hollering, "Hey, those girls jumped the fence!" I cringed and thought for sure a bouncer would come running over to toss us out on our ears. But, as luck would have it, no one in charge noticed. We were in.

The guys sitting around the fire pit were impressed with our brazen behavior. They called us over and offered to buy us drinks. The night was shaping up nicely—no cover charge and offers of free drinks. If the waitress wondered where my girlfriend and I sprang from, she didn't comment. Before long, we were sipping cold beers, watching the planes, and enjoying the conversation.

I was decidedly not interested in meeting a man that night. After four years of dealing with a difficult and insecure man-boy, I was thoroughly enjoying my independence and new-found freedom. I was dressed like a frump, sporting leggings, an oversized button-down oxford shirt, and olive-green army boots. I am quite certain that it was my blonde, statuesque friend Mary, with her miniskirt and legs up to her ears, who actually caught the group's attention. The best-looking guy in the group quickly latched on to her, and I was left to play the part of the unattractive, undesired tag-along friend. It was exactly what I had hoped for. And then I heard it—the scrape of a chair's legs against the cement patio. I looked up to see a male version of myself—the less attractive, tag-along friend—sidling up to me. I sighed. So much for a night without being hit on.

He was cute, if not as impressively good-looking as my girlfriend's catch of the day. He smiled at me, I smiled back, and we started talking. It turned out that we had landed in the middle of a group of pilots. All of the guys were flight instructors at the airport and had just gotten off work. I had never met a pilot before, and I'd never particularly cared to, but it did make for interesting conversation. Surprisingly, Evan was unimpressed when I informed him what I did for living. I believe his response was "Human Resources, what *is* that?" Despite my unattractive attire and the fact that he was unimpressed with my chosen career, he offered me his number. I gave him my number, with the caveat that I had recently freed myself from a long relationship, was thoroughly enjoying my newfound freedom, and was not at all interested in dating anyone at the moment. I kissed him on the cheek and jumped into Mary's car.

He called me anyway, a number of times. I didn't return his calls, but there was no Caller ID at the time, so I did actually pick up the phone once when he was calling We talked, he asked me out, I said no, and we hung up. A few weeks later, I was asleep on my couch at 7:30 on a Saturday night. I had a cold and was feeling punky. Evan called again and asked me out. I told him that I wasn't feeling well and wanted to stay home. He offered to come over and cook me dinner. Now that was sweet, really sweet, and it was something no one had ever offered to do for me before. It earned him my respect, and while I wasn't ready to let him come over to my apartment, I did drag myself into the shower and met him at a local club. We talked some more. I realized that I actually liked him quite a bit. He got a real kiss that night.

And so began the most significant relationship of my life. Eighteen years, two dogs, and two children later, we are still together. He still flies planes, although now they're Boeing 737s. He still doesn't understand what I do for a living. He still has my respect, and he has earned my love over the years. We made a life together, and it all started because I hopped that fence.

A Doubtful Christmas

The value of hard work, love, and commitment

Doyle Suit

URING THE SUMMER of 1944, my father sold everything we owned, took all the money, and disappeared
from our lives. My mother suddenly found herself alone to
care for five boys. I was the oldest, barely ten years old. My
youngest brother still wore diapers.

My grandparents welcomed us to their place—eighty acres
of rocky hill country twenty miles from the nearest town.
They scratched a living out of growing row crops in the thin
topsoil and running beef cattle on open range.

Grandpa butchered an extra hog that year, and we planted
a field of turnips to mature in the cool fall weather. We didn't
know a lot of different ways to prepare turnips, but the farm
supplied adequate food. My mother worked in the fields and
cared for us kids while I started fifth grade at school.

Changes in our lives couldn't be avoided. My father had
been abusive at times, but he'd always provided for us. Now
I worried about what might happen, but my mother stayed
positive, and assured us that she would keep us together as a
family and safe from harm.

Relatives donated hand-me-down clothes whenever they
could, and the farm produced enough food to nourish all of

us every day. I milked cows before catching the school bus and did chores after I got home each day. The younger boys washed dishes, fed chickens and pigs, and carried in firewood. Six-year-old Jerry was paired with me on a crosscut saw, and we regularly cut wood to heat the house during the winter.

Our efforts paled in comparison to what our mother did, however. At one hundred and five pounds, she could swing an ax, manhandle heavy horse-drawn plows, haul hay for the cattle, and harvest crops. Still, she found time to help us with homework and say prayers with the younger boys. She also made sure we attended church regularly, and taught us to appreciate music.

As Christmas approached, my mother didn't seem to smile as much. She hinted that Santa might have trouble bringing us presents this year. I considered myself practically grown, so I hid my disappointment, but when I overheard a conversation between my mother and grandma, I really started to worry.

"I can't afford to buy Christmas presents for the kids," my mother said.

"You need to have something for them," Grandma replied. "Maybe you could wrap some of the hand-me-downs."

"The kids would be terribly disappointed to find old clothes under the tree. I have to do better than that. Maybe I can make toys."

Homemade toys didn't excite me, but I realized she had no money to buy presents. Explaining that to the younger kids might be difficult, though.

One day my mother took a saw into the forest and returned with a stack of tree limbs. She left them in the harness room in the barn and refused to tell her curious children what they were for.

She worked on her project while I was in school, but I peeked when I had a chance. Pieces of wood had been cut into different shapes, then planed and sanded smooth. Later I found a stack of discs cut from a round oak limb. She also had started to carve a long piece of hickory, but I couldn't figure out its purpose.

She hid everything from us and frustrated my attempts to snoop. But I saw that she had used nails, glue, and paint from Grandpa's workshop. I concluded that she had to be making presents.

By Christmas week, my mother was her normal happy self again. Her project was apparently complete, and she'd kept it secret, because I'd looked everywhere without success.

When school let out for the holiday, my brothers and I cut a Christmas tree in the forest and dragged it home through the early snow. The whole family helped decorate it with ornaments, pinecones, and strings of popcorn. We gathered mistletoe and holly boughs and hung them throughout the house.

While my mother and grandma prepared food for Christmas dinner, I helped Grandpa with chores. The younger kids kept a diligent watch on pastries in the cupboard.

On Christmas Eve, we sang carols, and Grandpa read aloud from his Bible. After my mother shooed us off to bed, I lay awake for a long while, anticipating Christmas morning. Aunts, uncles, and cousins would come for dinner, and I was curious about what my mother's project would yield. I doubted that it could be anything elaborate, and homemade toys still didn't sound exciting, but I couldn't help noticing that she'd made a huge effort to provide for us.

I was already awake when she tapped on our door. "Merry Christmas, boys."

We hurried into the living room, and saw that a stack of packages had magically appeared overnight under the tree. But before we were allowed to investigate what Santa had brought, my mother herded us into the kitchen for breakfast.

We gathered around the tree a little later, and my mother handed out the presents. My brothers opened packages stuffed with brightly colored trucks, tractors, and trains. Those odd pieces of wood she had handled in secret were assembled and painted to form toys. The round discs made wheels that rolled, and the trucks and trains carried tiny logs and blocks. A tractor pulled a miniature wagon. The toys were beautifully crafted, and my siblings were thrilled.

When I tore off the newspaper wrapping my present, I found a hand-carved bow and a quiver of blunt arrows. Blunt was fine, because I knew how to make them suitable for hunting rabbits by forging steel arrowheads in Grandpa's shop.

Many difficult years would follow that particular Christmas, but I never again doubted my mother's ability to care for us. That Christmas would have been bleak without her skill and dedication, and it foretold her ability to provide for us. We were never hungry, and she made sure we got an education. She taught us faith in God and faith in our own abilities. That faith sustains me still.

Looking back, my mother's determination and perseverance changed the harsh reality of that time, transforming our
poverty into a memorable Christmas filled with delight. And
as it tuned out, the craftsmanship in those toys predicted her
later accomplishments as an artist and sculptor.

Sixty-three winters have come and gone since that special
holiday—that doubtful Christmas. I'm quite sure I've never
had a happier one.

Sweet Delights

Finding a sense of purpose

Lucy Parker Watkins

As told by Kim Loyd

I'VE ALWAYS BEEN a strong woman in every way—mentally, physically, and emotionally. I single-handedly reared my daughter and provided all that she needed. My friends and family have always known me to be a formidable force, openly expressing my opinions, working hard, and giving from my shallow pockets to secure the most basic of needs for others. Strength and faith have always been my greatest assets.

Eventually I married Tim, a wonderful man who stepped into our family as the perfect addition. Tim and I were only steps away from leaving the corporate world and starting our own specialty café. My life was nearly perfect, and each day I counted my blessings and gave thanks for all that I had.

Everything changed one sunny September day in 2005 when I awoke in a hospital room, unable to move. Tim stood before me, his eyes filled with tears as he stroked my hair. I was confused, but I recalled my car being upside down, the sound of helicopter blades, and a voice saying, "We're taking her to Methodist, not Parkland." Suddenly I was seized with a fear that life as I had known it was over. Would I have the future that I'd hoped for, or would I forever remain in need of others to provide basic care rather than being able to take care of them?

I remember driving home from the hairdresser that day before the accident. Dolled up in my favorite shorts and shirt with a great new hairdo, I was at my peak. Then I realized that I'd left my phone at the salon. I turned the car around and began heading back to get my phone. This little detour radically changed my life.

Suddenly, as though a person was sitting in the passenger seat next to me, I heard someone say, "Hold on! Don't move!" At that very moment, a car ran a stop sign and slammed into my car, sending it rolling over and over for nearly a hundred feet. The next thing I knew, the world in front of me was upside down. At the time, I had no idea that I had broken my neck in four places.

Had my car made another half roll and sat upright, I could have died. Any movement of my head would have severed my spine. The doctors didn't know what to expect in terms of my recovery, but they said that I was one lucky woman. Nobody was sure whether I'd walk again. Nobody could tell us what lay ahead for me other than several surgeries, transplanted cadaver bones, and a great deal of physical therapy.

To go from having everything I wanted to lying in bed unable to move, unable to take care of myself, was a nightmare. The thought of being a burden to my family whittled away at my spirit. My husband deserved more than a wife who needed constant care. My daughter deserved to have a strong mother. My grandchildren deserved a grandmother who could play games with them. And my mother deserved more than being on her knees praying for my life. I had to beat this, but I didn't how or whether I could. Nobody was sure.

Why did I survive?

There must have been a reason for my survival. Not knowing the answer was more painful than my physical injuries. All I knew for sure was that I had to heal. Otherwise the dream of our café might die. The dream of a true partnership with Tim would end, and he would be my nurse and my caregiver. I refused to be anything less than what he truly deserved. Although he always said that he would change my diapers until the day we were both in heaven, I wanted more for him than an invalid wife. I had to be a strong, happy mother and grandmother. Strength and reliability were essential to all that I had been, all that I hoped to be, and all that I was. My friends and family deserved more than the pained woman I had become.

Despite knowing that my survival was miraculous, depression was my constant foe. With only my ability to think and speak, I slowly began to realize that my purpose was to give love and hope to others. As I healed, it became apparent to me that I had to share my story as proof of the possibilities. But how? Where? I desperately needed answers.

Although my recovery was astounding, it left me physically challenged and unable to manage the duties of a café manager. Then a friend suggested that we open a popcorn and candy store. We believed that this new plan would save me the physical effort of running to and fro carrying piles of dishes in my arms. After ten years of planning, ten years of focus, and ten years of hope for our little café, it took only one day for us to decide to open the Mom and Popcorn Company.

Focused on our new venture, we set out to create a family place that would be like the candy stores from days gone by. It would be a place that encouraged the child within to come out and enjoy sweet temptations. Our new store was covered in rich woodwork and was made even more beautiful by natural light pouring through the oversized windows at the entrance. The walls were lined with wooden barrels and glass jars full of brightly colored candies. The overflowing stock of taffy, fudge, chocolates, gumballs, mints, and bottled sodas in an old-fashioned cooler brought hordes of customers to our little piece of Mayberry in North Texas. All we lacked was an outdoor rocking chair for Sheriff Taylor.

I didn't realize what this change in direction would afford me. Had we opened a café, I would never have been able to affect so many lives. Customers would merely have been hungry folks expecting superior service from a wait staff. Instead, customers come into our store out of curiosity rather than need. And the smiling faces of our fun-loving staff and the smell of freshly popped popcorn immediately greet them. Adults from all walks of life find themselves sharing memories of the moms and pops of their childhood. They bring with them their grandchildren and children, who ooh and ah over all the treats laid out before them. It's a place of fun and laughter, and it is my stage.

The atmosphere is disarming. Most people love all the colors, scents, and nostalgia of our little store. Occasionally, however, there are those who are unaffected by our staff or by all of the wonderful goodies we've set out. Those especially sad, serious faces always give me cause for concern. When prompted, I will share my story of survival. I'm always so deeply touched when I receive a call from a past customer who will share his or her story with me and thank me for taking the time to talk.

As I look back on the events that shaped my life, I realize that this store would not be here had I not been in the car accident. Although we reinvented our dream, I believe that it was for the best. I am witness daily to the renewed youth in the adults who come through our doors. Local children visit time and time again just because they feel safe with us. I encounter people of all ages, from all walks of life, and on whom I can have a positive effect.

My accident, as physically and emotionally devastating as it was, gave me a renewed sense of purpose.

My survival gave me the opportunity to fulfill my purpose, and our quaint popcorn and candy store has provided me with something I never would have had before the accident. It is a place where people come in for sweets and treats but leave with the knowledge that I am a friend who cares deeply about their lives. The bags of candy and popcorn under their arms are just icing on the cake.

Explosion

Tragedy has the power
to transform

Laura College

O N THE MORNING of April 18, 1995, Connie Mcphee
discovered that life is not without its subtle patterns.
Previously, she'd thought of her life as a random glitch in the
hard drive of humanity, an exception to the rule of predes-
tination. Brought up in a conservative household, raised to
believe in the power and might of the Lord, she nevertheless
felt that God had made a mistake when creating her.

She wasn't fat, ugly, dull-witted, cruel. She simply didn't
make friends easily, and her childhood was spent in front of
the television or with her nose buried firmly in a book. She
was awkward around her classmates because she was never
confident in her ability to say the right thing, so she chose
instead to avoid contact with her peers whenever possible.

Many children grow out of their awkward stages by the
time they hit puberty, but Connie still hadn't blossomed
when she made it to college. A freshman at Oklahoma City
University, she spent her evenings studying instead of watching television in the common areas, and although her suite
mates tried to include her in their activities, she declined each
time. Eventually, they stopped making the effort.

At 9:02 A.M. on that Tuesday morning, Connie was studying for a test in her dorm room when something shook the
building. Her first thought was *earthquake*, but of course
she lived in Oklahoma rather than Southern California. She
heard several students yelling down the hall and went to the
door to investigate, sure that a bulldozer or big truck had hit
the side of the dorm.

Instead, she found pandemonium in the halls.

The sound of sneakered feet pounding against linoleum
was nearly deafening. Usually the campus was quite silent
during the morning hours, when most students were in class,
but it seemed that every freshman and sophomore at the university had chosen that moment to flood her dorm.

For ten minutes or so, Connie made her way throughout
the building, seeking the source of the noise that had shaken
the walls. She asked several passing students if they knew what
had happened, but her voice was so quiet that few people took
notice. Finally, she retired back to her room and switched on
the small television set she'd brought from home. She heard
the following news flash. "Reports have confirmed a bombing at the Alfred P. Murrah federal building in downtown
Oklahoma City. Details are coming in as we speak, so stay
tuned."

Connie stared, riveted to the television screen, her eyes
trained on the images of death and destruction that the news-
casters had managed to feed from their helicopters. Smoke
and flames erupted from all sides of a building that she'd never
noticed before, although she did recognize the 200 block of
Fifth Street, where the bombing had occurred.

Classes were canceled soon after the OCU administration had been made aware of the situation, and students were encouraged to stay in their rooms. Every once in a while, a school employee would make his or her way down the halls of the dorms, carrying terrible news to a student who had lost a family member in the blast.

When one of the Dean's assistants knocked on the door to Connie's room, she and her roommate were sitting on their respective beds, watching footage of the rescue attempts. Firefighters, police officers, and K-9 unit dogs were scouring the wreckage, searching for living victims to save.

Connie stared blankly at the woman at the door, knowing that nobody in her family could possibly have been anywhere near the Alfred P. Murrah federal building during the time of the blast. Her parents lived in Coyle, which was nearly fifty miles north of Oklahoma City, and they never came to town on business. Her other relatives were scattered across the country with no business in OKC.

She happened to glance sideways at her roommate in that terrible moment when the woman in the doorway was unable to speak the news. Rhonda Howard, a thin slip of a girl who had previously appeared larger than life, had now shrunk back against her pillows as if hoping to fade into the material. She was usually vibrant, outgoing, quick to laugh and even quicker to poke fun; now she was stricken with what looked to be a mixture of horror and grief.

Connie knew.

Despite her lifelong desire to for anonymity, Connie instinctively slipped from her own bed to that of Rhonda's. She placed a gentle hand on the other girl's shoulder and nodded for the assistant to leave.

"Your dad?" Connie asked, reaching up to stroke Rhonda's hair. She'd heard snippets of conversation in the dorm about Mr. Howard's recent transition from the FBI to the Bureau of Alcohol, Tobacco and Firearms, which she figured had field offices in the federal building.

Rhonda nodded, her throat closed over with grief, and she leaned on Connie for support.

During the days that followed, Connie found within herself fresh reserves of strength and an almost instinctual urge to go to the aid of a friend in need. A friend—something Connie had never possessed before. Since classes were canceled for nearly two weeks, she was able to give Rhonda all of her time, and she even attended Mark Howard's funeral.

Thereafter, she and Rhonda were nearly inseparable, bonded by a friendship born of the mutual trust that can only develop during times of heartbreak. When Mark Howard's truck was delivered to Rhonda, its license plate melted but otherwise intact, Connie was by her side to take the keys.

Time heals all wounds, and eventually their friendship developed a foundation in other shared interests and wishes, but Connie would always remember Rhonda as the woman who had cracked her shell. It became easier for Connie to make friends with others, to immerse herself in campus life without the fear of rejection and desire for anonymity.

Tragedy, with all its pain and suffering, can sometimes transform into a life-changing moment that will inexplicably alter the course of one's life.

The Smiling Faces

The magic of musical pathways

Joseph Civitella

FROM A YOUNG age, Wanda was naturally gifted with an angelic voice and a temperament that allowed her to sing anywhere, any time, and without inhibition. As she matured into adolescence, she began to write her own music. "I get inspired," she would say. "It's like magic."

Breaking into the music business was a difficult proposition. Talent mattered, of course, but knowing the "right" people was essential. Wanda always heard the same question: "Do you really want to make it in the music business?"

Her answer never changed. "I'm ready to do whatever it takes, but I ain't gonna do anything it doesn't take."

Wanda had earned the little recognition she received through the sweat of her brow, playing mostly in dark and dingy bars to crowds of drinking men who hardly ever listened to her. Her efforts, though, served to give her the experience that would come in handy in her career.

Then one day she met Mark, a music agent, who took an immediate interest in her potential. "I can make a star out of you," he declared, "but you have to do what I tell you and not question my decisions."

"Yeah, okay," she answered, "but I want total freedom to let my music express itself."

"You look after your music," he instructed, "and I'll look after your career."

Although the arrangement seemed promising at first, Mark still booked her mainly in dark and dingy bars. The only difference was that she was paying him a booking fee.

"Welcome to the music business," another performer once told her. "Not only do you have to work harder for less money, you also have to trust that your agent is doing the right thing for you."

"How can you know that for sure?" she asked.

"You can't," came the reply. "And what's worse is that sometimes you're so worried that you begin to lose touch with your audience. You may as well pack your bags and go home at that point."

Wanda learned to "pay her dues and play her blues" and remain true to her art regardless of when or where the engagements occurred. But every once in a while, Mark booked her in an unusual place. "A nursing home?" she pleaded. "What am I going to do playing in a nursing home?"

"It's to mature your show," he replied. "If you can entertain a crowd of seniors who are usually falling asleep, you can hold any audience."

"But seniors are not my demographic, Mark."

"Precisely," came the curt reply. "Sing for my mom and her cohorts, and you'll thank me for it later."

So on a Sunday afternoon, Wanda played her guitar and sang to a gathering of seniors barely conscious enough to listen to her. After each song, she heard the staff applaud, but the residents were essentially unmoved. Try as she might, she felt as though she had failed to get through to them.

There was one resident who seemed transfixed by her. He was out of place in that nursing home because of his young age, but he also looked to be autistic. He was the only one who sang along with her.

After her show, Wanda found out from a nurse that Danny was diagnosed with a debilitating psychiatric illness that essentially cloistered him in his own mind. He happened to be sitting on a piano bench with his back to the piano. She went over to him, sat at the bench facing the piano, and played an old Beatles song. To her amazement, Danny sang to the music with a thin voice that was pitch perfect. She played other selections from the Beatles, and he knew them all as well.

Then Wanda played one of her original songs that she had earlier played on the guitar. To her astonishment, Danny knew all of the words and sang the song perfectly, even though he had heard it for the first time only minutes earlier. He had been looking straight ahead, never once turning to gaze at Wanda. But she saw him look at her from the corner of his eye, and she leaned back on the piano bench. That's when he smiled, just a little crack of the lips, but a smile nonetheless.

Wanda had gotten through to him, and he had returned the connection in his own inhibited way. One of the nurses noticed his smile and told Wanda that in six years she had never seen him smile even just a little. Wanda sat there quietly, emotionally moved. This was magic that went beyond music, yet it was she who was transformed by the experience.

Her heart jumped onto a different track that day. The business side of music simply didn't matter as much any more, now that she had discovered a therapeutic side that was much more important. She spent the rest of that afternoon playing the piano and singing with Danny. In fact, they played and sang until the early evening hours and provided an impromptu dinnertime concert for the nursing home residents and staff. The amount of applause didn't matter any more. What mattered was that more residents were smiling and singing along with her and Danny.

In the weeks following that show at the nursing home, Wanda found a new path for her talent and enrolled in a music therapy program. She also terminated her contractual arrangement with Mark because she no longer needed an agent.

"You're going into what?" he yelled on the phone.

"It doesn't matter *what*, Mark. The point is that I'm out of the music business."

"Don't think for a second that you could ever make your way back in if you change your mind! "

"And why not?"

"Because no one will touch you after what you've done to me."

"After what I've done to you? Tell me, Mark, weren't you the one who was supposed to make me a star? Or was it always more about your own reputation than my career?"

"I sent you to that nursing home to mature your act, not to destroy it!"

"And let me thank you, Mark, as you said I would, because now I've seen you for what you really are—an act."

Today Wanda heads up the music therapy program at the nursing home where she first met Danny. And she supervises young music therapy interns at other nursing homes owned by the same company. Aside from all the one-on-one sessions and group sessions she conducts, Wanda also organized a nursing home choir of musically challenged residents, whose smiles make every performance worthwhile in the end.

Danny is the lead singer in the choir, of course. He still doesn't look anyone in the eyes, but it doesn't matter because he smiles after each song. The choir is known as the "The Smiling Faces" Choir.

Losing Myself

My journey toward self-acceptance

Shaunna Privratsky

I LAUGHED AT MY mom's funeral. Please don't misunderstand; I loved her dearly. We said our goodbyes through a storm of tears, but I laughed when she went to her eternal rest.

She wasn't perfect, far from it. Mom couldn't pass a mirror without fretting about her weight or a bit of extra padding here and there. My mom never had an unkind word for anyone, yet she constantly disparaged herself, planting the seeds of discontent in my young mind.

I began to think that my developing body was getting fat as well. I loathed my body because I was not skinny enough, pretty enough, or popular enough. My body was different from those of the stick-thin models I saw in teen magazines. An inner critic was born then, a whiny voice in my subconscious detailing every fault, every flaw reflected in the mirror.

I went from a happy, well-adjusted child to a shy, self-critical teen. If I got a pimple, I was convinced that I was the ugliest girl to ever walk the planet. My widening hips and expanding bust line filled me with self-disgust. "Fat pig!" my inner critic proclaimed to my reflection. My friends assured me that I wasn't fat, yet I roiled in an inner sea of doubt.

I was the first to hit puberty in my class of two hundred. The rapid physical transformation of my body set me apart from my classmates. My large breasts were a constant source of embarrassment and private tears. I was branded a freak to all but my friends. I smiled through the insults, sniggers, and stares, but inside I felt like dying. Even when my female classmates "caught up," I still felt ostracized and ridiculed.

I developed a lot of unhealthy eating habits during that painful period. I would starve myself by skipping two or three meals and then overeat because I was so hungry. I was on a constant roller coaster of liking or hating myself according to the numbers on the scale. The problem was that the numbers were never low enough. I looked in the mirror and all I saw was a fat blimp.

I skated dangerously close to an eating disorder and eventually plunged over the edge. On Thanksgiving Day when I was thirteen years old, I forced myself to throw up for the first time. I immediately felt better. Bingeing and purging became a daily part of my life for the next twelve years. I even prayed to become anorexic —I thought that was the perfect solution to my constant weight fluctuations and bulimia.

I was searching for an identity connected to my looks. If I were skinnier, if I wore the right clothes and makeup, then maybe I would be accepted. Looking back at photos, I'm struck by the attractive girl in the pictures. I was never obese, and I was actually pretty, yet all I remember is the self-loathing and disgust that I wallowed in.

When I entered college, I desperately tried to quit my destructive eating habits. I would have succeeded had it been simply a matter of desire or willpower. However, not even realizing my goal of earning a degree in interior design could rid me of my bingeing and purging.

I dated my future husband, Wade, for five years before marrying him on June 1, 1991. I was gloriously happy on our wedding day. While I threw a glitch in the ceremony by fainting—I had forgotten to eat breakfast—the day turned out fine. We celebrated our first night as a married couple in blissful passion.

Then I locked myself in the bathroom and forced myself to throw up. I hadn't even eaten that much, yet I had such a compulsion to rid myself of unwanted calories that I threw up on my wedding day.

Wade never found out, then or later. I think my mom might have suspected my disorder when I was growing up, but she never confronted me. I was terrified of going to a dentist because I read that dentists are often the first to detect bulimia. The constant stomach acid bathing the teeth erodes the enamel and leaves telltale signs.

How much would my life have changed if I'd been found out? Would I have made more of an effort to quit? In hindsight, I think so. If my mom had said something, I would have been so ashamed and sad to have disappointed her that I might have been able to quit. At the very least, I could have sought counseling.

So, what finally got me to quit completely? I became pregnant with our first child in 1993. During those nine long months my mind underwent a transformation as dramatic as the changing shape of my body. But this time, I didn't mind the extra weight, my swollen ankles, or the unsightly stretch marks.

When Erica made her appearance in the world, I was truly at peace with my body for the first time in years. Her birth brought new meaning and purpose to my life. About the time I was coming to terms with my body, my mom called with the news that she'd found a lump in her breast. She bravely underwent chemotherapy and radiation for close to two years. We visited often, creating many joyful memories. The doctors finally declared her cancer-free, and my dad took her on a second honeymoon to Hawaii to celebrate her health and their twenty-fifth anniversary.

It seemed like a happy ending, but my mom's health took a turn for the worse. A few months after their fantastic trip, she was diagnosed with an incurable rare form of lymphatic cancer. Doctors gave her less than six weeks to live, but she defied all their gloomy predictions and lived for another year and a half.

In those few short years, we laughed and built a lifetime's worth of memories. My mother was able to meet my son Alex, born just after her devastating diagnosis. She watched him grow into a sturdy toddler. Her courageous spirit, as ethereal as a dandelion puff, held on long after her body gave out, until she was finally released at the age of fifty-one. I was twenty-nine.

I still miss her every day, and I always will. Her death taught me that life is a precious gift. If you don't enjoy it while you can, it melts away.

My mom's death gave new meaning to my life. Suddenly, it didn't matter so much when I spied my jiggly thighs. I decided I was not going to let a few extra pounds rule my life. My only regret is that I wasted so many years. If wishes were time machines, I would travel back in time and tell my thirteen-year-old self, "Believe in yourself. You are unique in your capabilities, your inner strength, and your dreams."

My days of suffering with bulimia are past me, forever I hope. My goal now is to help my fourteen-year-old daughter, Erica, through the strange and sometimes frightening passage from adolescence to womanhood. I don't want her to go through what I did.

I assure her that her body is perfectly normal, neither thin nor fat. We talk often about society's image of the "perfect" body. I point out that most girls her age aren't thin and that true beauty comes from within. I've shared with her my painful secret of my battle with bulimia.

My dream is that my daughter and I can finish growing together into beautiful strong women, proud of our bodies no matter what shape or size. If my mom could see us now, I am sure she would be proud. I must be content with the knowledge that I will hold a part of her in my heart forever.

When I think about my mom's funeral, I remember the scores of friends and family gathered to commemorate her passing from pain into perfect peace.

Knowing the end was near, she chose hymns she knew and loved for her memorial service. One song in particular brought laughter to my lips. The chorus was sung in two parts, pairing the deep low voices of the men with the high notes of the women.

It was as if Mom was standing beside me, giggling through the chorus the way we always had. So, in the midst of my sorrow over losing her, I laughed at my mom's funeral. Somehow, I am sure she laughed with me.

The Balloon

I lost my father, but found his love

Maris L. Franco

I GRADUATED FROM COLLEGE in the spring of 2004. It took me five years, not the four years I had hoped for, but, as I always told myself, what's important is that I did it. I had spent the last five years of my life going to school, working, and studying hard. Throughout that time, my father was one of my biggest supporters. It wasn't uncommon for me to be up at 3 A.M., poring over the history of Latin America or quantitative methods, when he came home from work. I can still clearly remember the light rap on the door. "Yes?" I replied, feigning annoyance, yet knowing full well who was there. Then, around the corner of the door frame, two huge brown eyes would appear. "Summa" was all he would say, walking away after flashing his trademark wink. Summa, or "Soooma," as my heavily accented Greek father would pronounce the word, was our private joke. It turned out that I was an exceptional student, and semester after semester, I would bring home As. My father, once valedictorian of his village school back home, had no hope of disguising his pride. "You keep this up and you know you will graduate *Summa Cum Laude*," he would say. To which I would always reply, "I can't guarantee As. I can just do my best. You're pressuring me!"

222

Of course, he only meant to be supportive, and I knew it. But somehow, pretending that he was the source of my pressure to maintain a perfect GPA gave me a bit of relief. He knew that I truly liked his confidence in me, and so year after year, despite all of my half-hearted complaints, he'd say, "I am always proud of you—As, Bs, Cs—but just imagine...Soooma!" Helpless in the face of his love and enthusiasm, all I could do was giggle.

One morning in the summer of 2003, my father had a sudden heart attack and died of congestive heart failure. I never got to say goodbye, but the last thing I said to him was "Good night. I love you." Many changes took place in my family during that time—too many to recount here—but I continued my studies, determined to graduate in May.

As the day of my graduation ceremony arrived, I was flooded with mixed emotions. This was the first of many big accomplishments that I would not be able to share with my father. Suddenly, my mind raced with images of the future— my first real job, my wedding day, my firstborn child—and I realized that I didn't want any of it. Unable to share my joy with him, what I wanted more than anything was not to graduate, but to make life stand still, so that the time since I had last seen him could not grow greater. I feared that my recollection of him would grow stale and hazy with age. I loved my father so dearly, and I simply could not imagine living so much of my life without him in it.

The president of my university called my name as I stepped on stage: "Maris Franco...*Summa Cum Laude*." This was the most bittersweet moment of my life, and something tells me that it always will be. As I walked across the platform to accept my degree, I turned to smile at my mother and sisters cheering for me in the audience. I could feel the tears begin to well up, but thankfully I was able to choke them back, reminding myself to be grateful for all that I still had.

That night, as I struggled with the balance between joy and sorrow over my big day, I stepped outside on my balcony to say a prayer. I hadn't planned on doing so, but I found myself praying, "God, please tell my father how much I love him. Thank you for giving me twenty-three years with him." Finally, before I went inside, I asked one more thing: "Please, God, give me a sign. I just want to know that he is okay."

About five minutes later, I remembered something I had left on the balcony. I walked back outside and could not believe what I saw! There, floating under the roof, was a shiny blue balloon. I looked around the apartment complex, but there was no one in view and no sign of a party or get-together. There seemed no way for the balloon to have gotten lodged out there. It was not a windy evening, and, what's more, the angle of the roof on that balcony made it virtually impossible for a balloon to float in from any direction. I turned the balloon and read the front. "Congratulations Grad." Beneath the words there was a small yellow star with two large eyes offering a loving wink. With that, the proverbial floodgates finally gave way to the pressure, and I was overtaken by the same emotions that I had so desperately choked back.

It was at that moment that I stopped doubting my father's continued presence in my life. I now know that he is with me, still taking pride in my accomplishments, rejoicing in my joys, and loving me unconditionally. At that moment, I realized that in matters of love and loss, if we hold firmly to love, then the latter never truly exists. I still have that balloon.

The World Is a Classroom

Our mentors in life are waiting to be found

Joseph Civitella

KEVIN WAS A freshman at university and was admitted into a general arts and sciences program. Although he could be a good student, he produced inconsistent grades. Sometimes he got an A+, sometimes a C-. He wanted to get into a professional program, like medicine, law, or architecture, but was worried that he didn't have the required marks.

Kevin was dedicated to doing the best that he could, and when he applied himself to something, he frequently succeeded. He spent a lot of time in the university library and took to heart the following words inscribed on one the walls: "Beholding the bright countenance of truth, in the quiet and still air of delightful studies."

One day he was waiting in line for one of the computer stations. Behind him stood an old man who appeared out of place in a university library. It wasn't just his age. While the vast majority of young students wore jeans and other casual attire, this elderly man was well dressed and used a cane. Perhaps he was a retired professor still doing some research. Or perhaps he was an academic of some sort.

Kevin heard a book drop on the floor behind him. He picked it up and handed it back to the old man. "Here you are, sir."

"Thank you, young man. My hands are not what they used to be."

Kevin nodded and faced the front of the line again.

"Not that they were anything other than hands before, you understand. It's just that age does strange things."

Kevin turned around to look at the old man. "That's okay. I don't mind."

"Neither do I. It's a fact of life that you'll begin to drop things."

Kevin smiled.

"At least I haven't dropped dead yet."

"That's a good thing."

"Yeah, I'd rather just drop a book." The old man snickered.

"Are you doing research?"

"Sort of. I thought I'd come back to university to find a wife."

"Excuse me?" Kevin couldn't help but laugh.

"Sure. You know, a rich young student who could take care of me."

"Really. I may want her for myself, though!"

"But you're not dropping anything yet."

Suddenly Kevin dropped his briefcase. Both he and the old man laughed.

"I like your sense of humor, young man. My name is Harold."

They shook hands. "My name is Kevin. It's nice to meet you."

They became fast friends, and saw each other frequently at the library over the ensuing weeks. Harold was a youthful and spirited eighty-one-year-old man. He spent his days at the university library, always reading a book or two and taking notes. He obviously loved to learn and was willing to talk about anything of interest.

While conversing about current events, Kevin took the opportunity to express his academic concerns to Harold. "I'm not really sure what I want to go into. One of the professional schools would be nice. But I might not have the grades to get in."

"Like what?"

"Architecture. Or medicine. Maybe law."

"No, I meant what kind of grades are you getting?"

"Oh. I've got a B– average so far this year."

"Why is that?"

"Well, I'm a good student, but…"

"But what?"

Kevin remained silent for a while. "Maybe I have to face the fact that I'm not smart enough."

"To get into one of those schools?"

"Yeah."

"Or not smart enough to get on in life?"

Kevin gave his friend a perplexed look. "What do you mean?"

"Let me ask you this." Harold's face was quite serious. "How important do you think a university education will be in your life?"

"Very important!"

"How?"

"It's my ticket to a profession."

"But I thought you said you might not be smart enough to get in."

"I might not."

"So what will you do if you don't get into architecture, medicine, or law?"

"I don't know. I guess I'll figure something else out."

"Like what?"

"I don't know yet." Kevin felt a little taken to task by his friend's tone.

"Let me ask you another way, then." Harold seemed to choose his words carefully. "Does a university education make you smart? Or does your smarts make a university education?"

Kevin laughed. "You're sounding the way my real grandfather might have sounded."

"Don't avoid the question." Harold remained serious.

"I suppose that smarts make a university education."

"Correct. In fact, your smarts can make your entire life, especially if you have the courage to make the necessary sacrifices."

"Okay."

"Just okay?"

"I … don't know what else to say."

"So then listen for a while longer, even if I sound like your grandfather." Harold sat up a little and cleared his throat.

"When I was your age, I never went to college. You know why? Because I went to war instead. The Second World War took my youth from me, and it almost took my life. And because of that I learned the most valuable lesson anyone can learn."

After a few moments of silence, in which Harold seemed to be holding back tears, Kevin prompted him.

"Something bad happened, right?"

"I had a mentor in the army. He was my immediate superior. His name was Jeff. He was a good man. Tough but fair."

Kevin sensed the pain in his friend. "You don't have to tell me, Harold."

"We were on the front lines. Bombs were exploding all over the place. Bullets were flying left and right. And we were caught in a bunker. We didn't know what to do. All of a sudden, an enemy trooper came up behind us. His gun was aimed directly at me. I froze. But Jeff…"

Kevin began to feel sad for his friend.

"Jeff threw himself in front of me, and took the bullet. The rest of us fired at the enemy trooper with everything we had. He was a goner. But so was Jeff. He died in my arms."

"I'm sorry, Harold."

"That bullet had my name on it. And from that moment on, I knew that if I ever got out of there alive, I would dedicate the rest of my life to making the best of each and every day. I suddenly realized that you never know when you won't be able to dodge the next bullet."

Kevin took Harold's story to heart and embraced him as his own mentor. Instead of worrying about academic prowess, Kevin began to focus on learning instead and allowed his interests to guide him. University became a forum in which to indulge one's interests. It was a means to an end, an end that had *no end*.

Two years after they met, Kevin enrolled in a joint history/ anthropology program and earned an honors degree. Today he is pursuing graduate studies in history and anthropology and intends on teaching at the university level.

Harold taught him that academia is great but that life is the best teacher. "Behold the bright countenance of truth in the quiet and still air of delightful learning."

The Happiest Day of My Life

Sharing my laughter and my life

Michael T. Smith

I T STARTED INNOCENTLY.
Many years ago, I worked in an office with large windows that looked out over a busy overpass. I was standing by one of those windows one day when a woman in a passing car looked up and made eye contact with me—naturally, I waved.

A chuckle escaped my lips as she turned and tried to identify me. It was the beginning of a year of window antics. When things were slow, I stood in the window and waved at the passengers who looked up. Their strange looks made me laugh, and the stress of work was washed away.

My co-workers took an interest. They stood back out of view and watched the reactions I received with amusement.

Late afternoon was the best time. Rush-hour traffic filled the overpass with cars and transit buses providing a wealth of waving opportunities for my end-of-day routine. It didn't take long to attract a following—a group of commuters who passed by the window every day and looked up at the strange waving man. There was a man with a construction truck who would turn on his flashing yellow lights and return my wave. There was the carpool crowd and the business lady with her children fresh from daycare.

My favorite was the transit bus from the docks that passed my window at 4:40 P.M. It carried the same group every day. They were my biggest fans.

Waving grew boring, so I devised ways to enhance my act. I made signs: "Hi!" "Hello!" "Be Happy!" I posted them in the window and waved. I stood on the window ledge in various poses; created hats from paper and file-folders, made faces, played peek-a-boo by bouncing up from below the window ledge, stuck out my tongue, tossed paper planes in the air, and once went into the walkway over the street and danced while co-workers pointed to let my fans know I was there.

Christmas approached, and job cuts were announced. Several co-workers would lose their jobs. Everyone was depressed. Stress reached a high point. We needed a miracle to break the tension.

While working a night shift, a red lab jacket attracted my attention. I picked it up and turned it in my hands. In a back corner, where packing material was kept, I used my imagination and cut thin white sheets of cloth like foam into strips and taped them around the cuffs and collar, down the front, and around the hem of the lab jacket. A box of foam packing and strips of tape became Santa's beard. I folded a red file folder into a hat and taped the beard to it. The whole thing slipped over my head in one piece.

The next day I hid from my co-workers and slipped into the costume. I walked bravely to my desk, sat down, held my belly, and mocked Santa's chuckle. They gathered around me and laughed for the first time in weeks.

A few minutes later, my supervisor walked through the door. He took three steps and then looked up and saw me. Pausing, he shook his head, turned, and left.

I feared trouble. The phone on the desk rang. It was my boss, and he grumbled, "Mike, come to my office!" I shuffled down the hall. The foam beard swished across my chest with each step.

"Come in!" The muffled voice replied to my knock. I entered and sat down. The foam on my beard creaked. He looked away from me. A bead of sweat rolled down my forehead. The only sound in the room was the hammering of my heart. "Mike..." That was all he managed to say. He lost his composure, leaned back in his chair, and bellowed with laughter as he held his stomach. Tears formed in his eyes, while I sat silent and confused. When he regained control, he said, "Thanks, Mike! With the job cuts, it's been hard to enjoy the Christmas season. Thanks for the laugh, I needed it."

That evening, and every evening of that Christmas season, I stood proudly in the window and waved to my fans. The bus crowd waved wildly, and the little children smiled at the strange Santa. My heart filled with joy.

For a few minutes each day, we could forget the job losses.

I didn't know it then, but a bond was forming between my fans and me. The next spring, I discovered just how close we had become.

My wife and I were expecting our first child. I wanted the world to know. Less than a month before the birth, I posted a sign in the window, "25 DAYS UNTIL 'B' DAY." My fans passed and shrugged their shoulders. The next day the sign read, "24 DAYS UNTIL 'B' DAY." Each day the number dropped, and the passing people grew more confused.

One day a sign appeared in the bus, "What is 'B' DAY?" I just waved and smiled.

Ten days before the expected date, the sign in the window read, "10 DAYS UNTIL BA-- DAY." Still the people wondered. The next day it read, "9 DAYS UNTIL BAB- DAY," then "8 DAYS UNTIL BABY DAY." My fans finally knew what was happening.

By then my following had grown to include twenty or thirty different buses and cars. Every night, they watched to see if my wife had given birth. The number decreased and excitement grew. My fans were disappointed when the count reached "zero" without an announcement. The next day the sign read, "BABY DAY 1 DAY LATE." I pretended to pull out my hair.

Each day the number changed, and the interest from passing traffic grew. My wife was fourteen days overdue before she finally went into labor. Our daughter was born the next morning. I left the hospital at 5:30 A.M., shouted my joy into the morning air, and drove home to sleep. I got up at noon, bought cigars, and appeared at my window in time for my fans. My co-workers were ready with a banner posted in the window:

"IT'S A GIRL!"

I didn't stand alone that evening. My co-workers joined me in celebration. We stood and waved our cigars in the air as every vehicle that passed acknowledged the birth of my daughter. Finally, the bus from the docks made its turn onto the overpass and began to climb the hill. When it drew close, I climbed onto the window ledge and clasped my hands over my head in a victory pose. The bus was directly in front of me when it stopped in heavy traffic, and every person on board stood with their hands in the air.

I was choked with emotion as I watched them celebrate my new daughter.

Then it happened—a sign popped up. It filled the windows and stretched half the length of the bus. "CONGRATULA-TIONS!" it read.

Tears formed in the corners of my eyes as the bus slowly resumed its journey. I stood in silence as it pulled away from view. More fans passed. They tooted their horns and flashed their lights to congratulate me. I hardly noticed them as I pondered what had just happened.

My daughter had been born fourteen days late. Those people must have carried that sign for weeks. Each day they must have unrolled it and then rolled it back up. The thought of them going through so much just to celebrate my new baby made me cry.

I made a fool of myself in that window for eight months. I made those people smile after a long day at work. They must have enjoyed it, because on the happiest day of my life they showed their appreciation.

That day, more than twenty years ago, changed me. I just wanted to make my day better. I didn't realize how it affected others.

Ever since then, I try to put a smile on someone's face every day. I compliment strangers on their clothing. I start conversations in elevators. I even make jokes in crowded New York City subways. Some may think I'm stupid, but I know there is a chance that I'm making someone's day—someone who may one day hold up a sign that says "Congratulations!"

Afterword

Flutters of Change

Peter Sacco, Ph.D.

IN THE MOVIE that bears his name, Forrest Gump says, "Life is like a box of chocolates. You never know what you're gonna get." He wasn't a pop psychologist by any measure; some people might say that he is an American icon but his words are profound and still ring true today. Life comes our way whether we are ready for it or not, and it brings to us a variety of experiences. These experiences will be different for everyone, but they will all have one thing in common...*perception*!

Aha! Eureka! Have you ever had one of those moments of enlightenment that totally immobilized your entire being? Surely you have. It's as if you were frozen in a time warp, living a profound single moment that perhaps didn't feel so important then. Or maybe it did, but at the time you couldn't imagine the magnitude it would assume later on in your life. Have you ever looked back on an experience and "just got it"? The experience may have been like a puzzle, jumbled and unclear. It may have been a moment of confusion, despair, frustration or even disappointment.

Some great thinkers assert that everything happens for a reason, and that it is usually for the best. How could an experience that challenges us happen for the best? If someone told you this to your face, you might think they were trying to minimize your pain or that they were crazy!

Do you have any regrets?   Are you a "would have, could have, should have" thinker? Do you wish you could hop in a magical time machine and go back in your life to change the past? In retrospect, can you see those forks in the road?

Did you play it safe and take the path of least resistance? Or did you leap onto the road less traveled, trusting your instincts, and taking one step at a time? Decisions, decisions, decisions! Guess what? Choices and opportunities are always present.

Welcome to Your Thin Threads moment!

William James, considered the father of American psychology, was once quoted as saying, "It is only by risking our persons from one hour to another that we live at all. And often enough our faith beforehand in an uncertified result is the only thing that makes the result come true." *Thin Threads* are the lifelines that connect us to our destinies. They are the bridges that help us cross from where we were to where we are now and where we want to be. They are the spiritual intertwinings that connect us to people, places, and things. *Thin Threads* are the decisions that get us through challenging moments—the forks in the road of life, the dark moments when our vision is reduced—when we stand at the edge of a cliff and wonder what's next. They prepare us for what's around the bend. Thin Threads are the intuitions and extrasensory insights, or the "gut feelings," that prove hindsight is always crystal clear!

For some people, the greatest discomfort they will experience is looking back on their lives, because the regret is just too painful. Sure, many psychologists and theorists maintain that looking back on one's past is useless because you can't change things. But what if you examine the past like an archeologist who connects time periods using artifacts? What if you think of the past and present as a school that offers you life lessons and your artifacts as tools that prepare you for where you really want to go and who you really want to be? Suddenly the past doesn't seem all that bad or useless. It can be used like GPS to get you to your desired destination. As a matter of fact, it can lead you to finding the real you!

Most people look at their lives and see only "points of interest." They notice where they were and where they are now. They direct their attention to points A, B, C, etc. It is within the connections between points A, B, and C that true living happens. These connections are the *thin threads* that help you navigate the course of your life and steer you in the direction you need to go. It is the process of living that matters most!

As Albert Einstein magnificently put it, "Imagination is everything. It is the preview of life's coming attractions." Inspired decision-making is connected to *Thin Threads*, and *Thin Threads* lead you to your destiny! Did you know that anything worth achieving and experiencing originates from inspired thought? What is inspired thought? It is the ability to imagine things as you would like them to be and then to go out and live your life accordingly. Remember, thoughts always produce feelings. You can't feel anything unless you first think it. And once you start to feel something, it stirs life... it calls action into place!

Imagination is the key because imagination involves thought. Therefore, great imaginations invoke powerful feelings that lead to extraordinary outcomes—dare we say the perfect recipe for *Thin Threads*?

Everyone has a unique story to tell. Not everyone enjoys celebrity status, but guess what? We're all equal, and we all possess the same potential for our own unique success. The only advantage one person holds over another is the power of his or her imagination and the motivation of the inspired thoughts; which invariably lead that person to his or her destiny. Some dare to live on the edge, dare to defy the status quo, instead of trying to achieve perfect balance in their life. Who wants absolute balance? If something is in perfect balance, it may feel comfortable, but perfect balance also means that it isn't moving or changing. If your life isn't getting you to where you want to go, it may be because you're too busy stabilizing yourself on a high wire. Get moving instead!

Do you remember those wonderful television shows like *Touched by An Angel*? They portrayed how angels were on the outside looking in, helping people get to where they were meant to be. You might even say that the angels held the *thin threads*, helping people take off like kites catching a gust of wind and reaching for the heavens.

Clichés are often used when it comes to explaining dreams or accounting for success. Unfortunately, they are often misconstrued and never fully appreciated for what they really are—valuable life lessons. You will hear sayings such as "When one door closes another one opens," "Follow your heart," or "Listen to your gut."

Do you know what all these clichés have in common? You guessed it—they are all *Thin Threads*! When people cast them aside due to cynicism or disbelief, they overlook awesome opportunities for learning and living. Instead of veering off the main road of life and following their dreams, they park and let life pass them by. Those who understand the message behind the clichés are truly of a proactive mindset and can be heard saying, "If it's going to be, then it's up to me!" They strive not to cave in to negativity or express a passive excuse such as "It wasn't meant to be."

Each setback you experience offers you a new opening to pursue your dreams. When you begin thinking this way, the world opens up for you!

According to a June 2008 *Boston Globe* feature, MIT meteorologist Edward Lorenz watched his work become a catch phrase. Lorenz, who died in April 2008, created one of the most beguiling and evocative notions ever to leap from the lab into popular culture: the "butterfly effect," the concept that small events can have large, widespread consequences. The name stems from Lorenz's suggestion that a massive storm might have its roots in the faraway flapping of a tiny butterfly's wings.

Translated into mass culture, the butterfly effect has become a metaphor for the existence of seemingly insignificant moments that alter history and shape destinies. Typically unrecognized at first, they create threads of cause and effect that appear obvious in retrospect, changing the course of a human life or rippling through the global economy. There are many butterflies out there. A tornado in Texas could be caused by a butterfly in Brazil, Bali, or Budapest.

In retrospect, while close examination can reveal cause and effect, as humans we cannot predict the ultimate outcome of our actions. "It's impossible for humans to measure everything infinitely accurately," says Robert Devaney, a mathematics professor at Boston University. "And if you're off at all, the behavior of the solution could be completely off." When small imprecision matters greatly, the world is radically unpredictable. Realistically, we can't know.

We all expect the world to be comprehensible, expect that everything happens for a reason and that we can pinpoint all those reasons, however small they may be.

But, according to Devaney, "nature itself defies this expectation..."

Thin Threads moments are those imperceptible changes that can affect your life in ways you never expect. So however small they may be... pay attention to the *flutters of change*!

Peter Andrew Sacco, Ph.D., is an author, psychology professor, and former private practitioner in Canada. He is an international lecturer on psychology/self-help related topics.

Contributors—Our Thin Threaders

Manette Adams   discovered the fun of writing as a shy twelve-year-old. This life-long interest was inspired by a birthday gift—a red leather diary. She graduated from Hollins College, and received her M.A. from Yale University. Ever interested in third-world problems, in 1979 Manette helped Vietnamese families settle in this country. Today she lives in a retirement community in Hamden, Connecticut, with her husband of 59 years.

Lisa Arneth   is a wife and mother of two beautiful children. Born in Oklahoma, she is a bit of a gypsy and has lived in New York City, New Jersey, and Vermont. Currently she calls Connecticut home. Although she has always enjoyed writing, she works as a Human Resources professional in her day job. She spends her off hours reading, running, and wrestling with her bulldog, Maximus. Although she has been married to a pilot for thirteen years, she still gets a little nervous during takeoffs and landings.

Ana Barlow   was born in Russia, where she spent part of her childhood in an orphanage until an American family adopted her at the age of ten. She currently attends the University of North Texas, where she is majoring in sociology. One day she hopes to better the international adoption system and help the many other orphans in need of families.

Sylvia Bright-Green   has been published in five books during her twenty-eight-year writing career, and she has sold manuscripts to over 1,500 newspapers and national magazines.

Jennifer Bunin   received a B.A. in English from Wesleyan University, in Connecticut, in May 2009. She was an editor and contributor to Wesleyan's literary and art magazine, *Ostranenie*, where she published much of her own poetry. She is looking forward to a career that will allow her to use her literary skills and continue writing. She enjoys traveling, music, and staying involved in the political landscape of America.

Arnold Carmel   was raised in Great Britain in a left-wing family. At the age of 18 he emigrated to Israel, and after serving in the Israel Defense Forces, he became a member of a kibbutz. After leaving the kibbutz, Arnold and his wife came to the U.S., where he received two degrees, in psychology and education, and then received his Ph.D. in educational psychology. Over the next 40 years Arnold worked in the fields of

CONTRIBUTORS

secular and Jewish education. He is the proud father of two daughters and six grandchildren.

Joseph Civitella* Msc.D., writer and line editor for *Thin Threads* stories, is a lifelong student of spiritual metaphysics—the quest for truth, meaning, and purpose. Along with his Ph.D. in metaphysical sciences, Joseph is an ordained minister. His writing credits include the novel *Shadows of Tomorrow*, a compilation of poems and prose called *The Blossoming*, and a CD of original songs named *Soulace*. He operates the School of LifeWork, based on his nonfiction book *Turning your Passion into a Profession*. Additional information on Joseph can be found at:

Joseph@SchoolofLifeWork.com
www.SchoolofLifeWork.com
www.MySpace.com/SchoolofLifeWork

Laura College is a freelance ghostwriter and aspiring novelist from Houston, Texas. She has written more than twenty books for businesses across the United States, publications that range from educational fables to business how-tos. She has also been published in several national magazines

---

* Special thanks to Joseph Civitella, whose dedication to the stories of people and efficient work in rewriting some of the *Thin Threads* stories have been invaluable to this project!

and trade journals, and is currently hard at work on her first suspense novel.

Dylene Cymraes   has had a love affair with the written word since she discovered the escape of a good book as a child. Life has taken her all over the United States and Europe. She has written two novels and a biography, and she currently writes and edits screenplays. She is married, has four children and four grandchildren, and lives in western Maryland.

Deborah DeNicola   is the author of five poetry collections. Her spiritual memoir, *The Future That Brought Her Here*, was published in 2009. Her sixth book of poetry, *Original Human*, is scheduled for publication in 2010. Deborah edited the anthology *Orpheus & Company: Contemporary Poems on Greek Mythology*, from The University Press of New England. Among other awards, she received a Poetry Fellowship in 1997 from the National Endowment for the Arts.

Claudia D'Souza   is a freelance writer and former reporter who lives in Oakville, Ontario. Claudia has worked in every aspect of journalism, from newspaper, magazine, and news-letter writing to public relations and communications. Her specialty is stories about people of all kinds.

Maris L. Franco   holds a degree in psychology but became disillusioned with some aspects of the profession and chose not to pursue it further. Currently she works for a heavy construction firm, managing the office. She handles everything from correspondence and insurance claims to travel arrangements and event planning. She has always considered herself a writer, and it has been a lifelong passion. She became serious about pursuing writing professionally about two years ago, and is now determined to do so. This career path is the only one she sees herself on, as writing makes her happy.

Leslie Galiker's   nonfiction and fiction have been published in various magazines. Leslie feels that her life experiences as a daughter, wife, mother, grandmother, and friend have given her an abundance of writing fuel. She is a former reporter and has been a medical transcriptionist for 18 years. Leslie shares her home in Jackson, New Jersey, with two teenage cats.

Bethany Garfield   is a freelance journalist and aspiring author who specializes in narrative nonfiction. Currently she is working on a book about the lives of New Orleanians following Hurricane Katrina. She sometimes dabbles in fiction as well. For the time being, Bethany is living in New York, where she enjoys taking long walks with her dog and eating pumpkin pie with her boyfriend, Aaron. She plans to return to New Orleans in the near future.

Amber Gillet   is a working mom who resides in Rutland, Massachusetts, with her husband, four sons, and two Labs, also boys. In her words, "I'm definitely outnumbered!"

Elizabeth Anne Hill   is the author of three books: *Twin Souls: A Message of Hope for the New Millennium*, co-written with her twin sister, Catherine, in spirit; *The Circle of Life*; and *The Gift*, inspirational books for children (www.twinsoulsonline.com). Elizabeth is the co-creator of a 3-CD set called *An Interview with the Universe*, (www .interviewwiththeuniverse.com). She also guides travelers to sacred and powerful places around the world (www .sacredsitejourneys.com).

Kate Kowsh   is a 26-year-old University of Florida graduate. She is a freelance journalist who chooses to write as a way to locate and project the commonalities that bind each of us.

Delores Liesner   credits her Native American heritage for the gifts of storytelling and childlike wonder of life. Delores enjoys sharing the joys, hope, and adventure of a personal relationship with God—loved by the Father, lifted by the Son, led by the Spirit. Despite an abusive childhood, she emerged an energetic woman of faith who wears many hats. She is passionate about her role as a wife, a mother, and a hyper-grandma. Delores welcomes contact at lovedliftedandled@wi.rr.com.

Leslie Martini   is a freelance writer living in Marblehead, Massachusetts, with her husband and two daughters, Allison and Olivia. Leslie's work has been published most recently in the Boston Globe's *Lola* magazine and *North Shore* magazine. In addition to freelance writing, Leslie works for Fraxa Research Foundation, a parent-run non-profit whose goal is to fund research toward effective treatments and a cure for Fragile X Syndrome.

Barbara Elisse Najar   is a freelance writer whose essays have been published in the *Washington Post* and local newspapers. She was a speechwriter and healthcare writer for the federal government, specializing in substance abuse and other healthcare issues. Barbara is currently working on a book about animals and studying to become a telepathic animal communicator. She has a master's degree in public health and a bachelor's degree in English.

Susan Lynn Perry   is an accomplished writer and frequent contributor to the *Thin Threads* and *Cup of Comfort* series. Along with authoring numerous articles, short stories, novels, and nonfiction books, she is most recently the author of *Mother Cub*, an uplifting account of the challenges and

joys involved in helping her young son emerge from autism. Ms. Perry can be reached through her website www
.mothercub.com.

Shaunna Privratsky   laughs at the extra ten pounds she
would like to lose. Luckily, her full-time job as author and
caretaker of her disabled husband doesn't require a stick-thin
figure. She enjoys reading trashy novels, trading surly looks
with her two teenagers, and remodeling a bathroom. Please
check out her website The Discount Diva and sign up for her
free newsletter at http://shaunna67.tripod.com/id21.html.

L.J. Reed   writes full time from her retirement home in Port
Aransas, Texas. L.J. has been published previously in *Reader's
Digest* and *Woman's World*, and she has won two firsts, two
seconds, and numerous other prizes in writing competitions.
Reed has also completed three novels, but publication has
eluded her so far.

Julie Adler Rosen   has been writing short stories since
childhood. She studied English and art history at UC Berke-
ley and received her M.S.W. from USC. While her passion/
hobby is writing and painting, her truest joy is raising her sons
and spending time with her husband. Her daily goal is to be
in the moment and laugh as often as possible.

Mary I. Russo   considers faith her most valuable asset. As wife, mother, and involved grandma, she evolved from childcare provider to writer of short stories. She blended poetry with photography in her work *The MIR Collection*. In 2000, Mary shared her vision of the Blessed Mother in *Through A Child's Eyes of Faith*. Her goal is to touch as many lives as possible with love and understanding, for as long as God gives her.

Joyce M. Saltman   is by no means a new kid on the block. She has charmed and tickled the hearts of students and business audiences for over 20 years. As a friend of hers would say, "Joyce is world famous in Connecticut (and now Florida!)." Joyce is known as the Laughter Guru. She holds many advanced degrees, but her down-to-earth professorship at Southern Connecticut State University and her speeches at business conferences as far as Tokyo have given her a broad laughter base! Her newest book, a satire on kids going to college, is published by Kiwi Publishing, and is titled *I'm Changing the Locks & Cementing the Windows: Preventing the Boomerang or How to Keep the Kids from Coming Back*.

Michael T. Smith   is a part-time writer and full-time project manager in telecommunications. Michael believes his true calling is writing from the heart and thinks it is important to share a smile, a wave, a kind word, and a tear. His life experiences have given him a special heart, which shows in his writing. His stories have appeared in newspapers in both Canada and the U.S. and in various online publications.

Dorothy Stephens is a former teacher and a freelance writer whose work has appeared in the *New York Times*, the *Miami Herald*, the *Los Angeles Times*, *Adventure Cyclist*, *The World and I*, the *Larcom Review*, and other national publications. She co-authored the book *Discovering Marblehead* and was a finalist in the 1997 Bread Loaf Bakeless Creative Nonfiction competition. She and her husband live in Marblehead, Massachusetts.

Doyle Suit and his wife of fifty years live in St. Charles, Missouri, near their children and grandchildren. They dance, play golf, and travel. Doyle plays and sings bluegrass music for fun. His work has appeared in *Good Old Days Magazine*, the *St. Louis Suburban Journals*, *Storyteller Magazine*, *Spring Hill Review*, *Sweetgum Notes*, *Cuivre River Anthology*, and other publications.

Kathy Shiels Tully launched both her writing life and her married life by proposing to her now-husband in the *Boston Herald's* op-ed on Leap Day 1996. Her daughters, Bridget and Katie, are dreams come true. In addition to *Thin Threads*, Shiels-Tully is the former "People" columnist for the *Melrose Free Press*. Her work is also published in *Chicken Soup for the*

Often we meet our destiny on the road we take to avoid it.